Preface

This book takes the Holy Bible as God's Word and seeks to draw from it lessons on leadership. At the same time, like other volumes in Concordia's Leadership Series, I will apply here what we might call "First Article knowledge" to leadership processes in the church. This kind of knowledge comes from researchers who study the world God created. While it is not theology drawn directly from the Bible, it is truth that can support and augment theology. Over the past six decades or so, scholars in organizational studies have developed many ideas helpful to those who lead God's people. Built on sound principles of psychology and sociology, leadership theory can guide those who want to lead others with skill and courage.

Some in the Christian community have rejected all organizational theories because some scholars' ideas clash with the truths revealed in the Holy Scriptures. When theories contradict Holy Scripture, we must reject them. They are dangerous to faith and life in the body of Christ. Yet while filtering out the "camels" and even the "gnats" Jesus warned us about (Matthew 23:24), Christian leaders will want to take advantage of ideas and methods that can strengthen their leadership skills and abilities. Our Lord wants to equip us in every way "with everything good for doing His will," even as He works in us "what is pleasing to Him" (Hebrews 13:21). He does this, in part, through "First Article" truths.

This book presents one model for leaders in the church—servant leadership. Though I see it as congruent with Scripture and worthy of study, other models also grace the pages of the Holy Scriptures. I pray that this brief study will encourage others to explore what Scripture has to say about leadership in the church. I also pray that it will provoke Christian leaders to dig into more of the organizational scholarship that is available to us.

God wants His people to be not only well-fed but well-led. Every leader in the church I have ever known has wanted to lead God's people well. May God grant us wisdom to discern the truth about leadership—wherever we may find it. And may He grant us grace to apply that truth for the good of the church and the glory of our Savior!

servant LEADERSHiP

Setting Leaders Free

Jane L. Fryar

CHRISTIAN LEADERSHIP SERIES

CONCORDIA PUBLISHING HOUSE · SAINT LOUIS

Copyright © 2001 by Jane L. Fryar
Published by Concordia Publishing House
3558 S. Jefferson Ave., St. Louis, MO 63118–3968
1-800-325-3040 • www.cph.org

All Scripture quotations, unless otherwise indicated, are taken from the Holy Bible, New International Version®. NIV®. Copyright © 1973, 1978, 1984 by Biblica, Inc.™ Used by permission of Zondervan. All rights reserved.

Scripture quotations marked NKJV™ are taken from the New King James Version®. Copyright © 1982 by Thomas Nelson, Inc. Used by permission. All rights reserved.

Manufactured in the United States of America

5 6 7 8 9 10   20 19 18 17 16 15 14 13 12 11

Contents

Preface   5

1. Servant Leadership   7

2. Service First!   20

3. Servant Leaders See Deeply   32

4. The Power of Persuasion: Community
   and Consensus   45

5. Stewardship of God's Gifts   61

6. Growing and Healing   78

Appendix   96

Notes   101

References   105

1

Servant Leadership

How do leaders do what they do? What does Bill Gates have in common with Mother Theresa, for example? Why do some people with no official recognition or title attract a loyal following, while others lead in title only? Questions like these have fascinated people for a long time. Centuries before Christ, Plato wrote about leadership in *The Republic*. Despite this long history, scholars did not begin to study leadership in a scientific way until recently. Over the past five decades, theorists have examined various pieces of the leadership puzzle—leader traits, leader behaviors, and the effects that various contexts or contingencies exert on leaders and followers.

After examining the components, leaders in the real world of Monday morning's e-mail and Friday evening's traffic jam need ways to put the puzzle back together again. They need practical direction in leadership. As hierarchical approaches to leadership disappear in business and society in general and as organizations shift away from top-down, autocratic modes of leadership, leaders need to understand how to optimize new models of organizing. Leaders need to know how to build consensus, how to motivate followers, how to improve the quality and caring of our institutions. The theories and concepts of *servant leadership* can help.

Servant leadership takes a holistic view of the relationship between leaders and followers and the tasks they share. It takes into account the externals of leadership traits, behaviors, and circumstances. But it is rooted in the identity of the people to whom others look for leadership. It particularly focuses on the core beliefs and values leaders hold and cherish.

From the Upper Room to the Board Room

In one sense, the terms "servant" and "leader" seem paradoxical, and "servant leadership" seems to be an oxymoron. Yet how crisply the term captures the earthly life and mission of our Lord Jesus: "I am among you as the One who serves" (Luke 22:27, NKJV). Remarkable words—especially when we consider who spoke them and when. It was Holy Thursday. The next day the Romans would lead a young Galilean preacher out to Calvary's hill. There He would lie down on a rough-hewn cross, stretch His arms out wide, and die in an act of service that even now defies human understanding.

Jesus' followers expected something quite different from Him. Their religious leaders demanded titles of reverence and respect. Their business leaders expected to be wined and dined, waited on hand and foot. Their political leaders pushed others around, taking full advantage of their positions of power. Jesus' disciples wanted exactly that kind of power and honor for themselves. A few moments before Jesus explained His own servanthood that night, His disciples had engaged in an ugly spat over which one of them most deserved the highest position in the coming Kingdom (Luke 22:24–29).

Many today likewise misconstrue the idea of leadership. Some in the church load it with connotations of supremacy, privilege, and power. Perhaps we covet positions of leadership so that we can have our own way or so that others will honor us. Perhaps our love of power reveals our sinful nature, ever rebelling against our Lord. But today Jesus still lives among us as "the One who serves." He not only modeled a better way of life and of true leadership for us; He sacrificed Himself on the cross and rose again to remove the guilt of our selfishness and sinful pride. Through Word and Sacrament He is even now remaking us in His own image, creating within each of us a servant's heart, a heart of compassion and love just like His own (Ephesians 2:4–10).

The idea of servant leadership really goes all the way back to God's Old Testament people. Kings in ancient Israel were often called "shepherds." The Lord held them responsible to serve His people, to protect, guide, instruct, and cherish their subjects, not to lord it over them or to "fleece the flock," so to speak. (See Jeremiah 23:1–8.) But not even the Old Testament fleshed out the concept in all its fullness. To get the fullest picture of servant leadership, God's people had to wait until God Himself took on human flesh to live and die among us.

In Jesus, humanity finally saw with its own eyes what true servant leadership is like (Philippians 2:5–11).

Deep Identity

What *is* servant leadership? Advocates in the business world have noted with some degree of dismay that people often press them for a quick explanation of the concept. "That may not be possible," Don Frick, an expert on servant-leadership issues, notes, "because [servant leadership] describes a process of inner growth and outer consequences that, though based on some universal principles, must necessarily take unique expression within particular individuals and institutions. . . . [When] servant leadership is reduced to a collection of admirable qualities and learned skills that are displayed in organizational settings, it is all too easy to forget that servant leadership is, first, about deep identity" (p. 354).

Robert Greenleaf was the first to popularize the term "servant leadership" and set down its foundational concepts. Servant leadership was indeed a part of his own "deep identity." Greenleaf, a highly placed executive at AT&T for much of his adult life, made advocacy for servant leadership a kind of second career. At age 66, he wrote an article calling attention to servant leadership and its power. The article struck a chord with many readers, and, until his death in 1990, Greenleaf continued to promote servant leadership, teaching managers to practice it and challenging organizations to adopt it as they related to workers, clients, suppliers, and customers. Still today the Greenleaf Center for Servant Leadership continues to promote his ideas.

While few would agree with everything Greenleaf proposed, no one can deny that his personal credibility helped to ignite a blaze of interest in servant leadership. Until recently, few scholars had studied the results of servant leadership in organizations. Researchers have now begun to gather evidence of its effectiveness. Ross Stueber, former director of school ministry for The Lutheran Church—Missouri Synod, has shown a strong correlation between servant leadership and positive outcomes in Lutheran high schools headed by servant leaders.

The essence of servant leadership springs not from a leader's traits (e.g., kindness) or behaviors (e.g., goal setting). At its heart, servant leadership is identity-based. The servant leader's core identity and core values determine his or her attitudes and actions. Greenleaf warned that if we start with behaviors, enlarging them to mask our true identity, we have only a gimmick. We lose our authenticity—and followers always know it! As Frick has noted, the concept of servant leadership remains somewhat ambiguous, and its values defy definition by sound byte.

This helps explain the variety in the lists of servant-leader behaviors and attitudes drawn up by those who have attempted to describe the approach. In the course of working on this study, I collected more than 50 terms used to describe servant leaders, their values, attitudes, beliefs, and approaches toward followers. Most of the behaviors and attitudes cluster around five values.[1] I will detail and defend the theological and organizational foundations for each of these value clusters in the chapters that follow. The list below simply introduces them:

- Servant leaders place a premium on service. This partly involves helping followers attain their own personal goals. Servant leaders also want to serve in such a way that their organizations thrive for the good of all organizational stakeholders and society in general. Both the individual member and the organization benefit from the leader's service.

- Servant leaders want each follower to live a life of significance and purpose. They use their intuition, experience, foresight, and insight to cast an encouraging, uplifting, and compelling vision of the future that energizes followers. Servant leaders focus followers' efforts on worthwhile goals, and they affirm and encourage followers.

- Servant leaders value the freedom and dignity of the individual. They rely on the art of persuasion to create consensus and community, instead of forcing compliance.

- Servant leaders want followers fully to develop their gifts and abilities. They are stewards of followers' gifts, appreciating their strengths and helping them develop and use their abilities. Servant leaders take risks by empowering others because they know that this ultimately strengthens organizations and brings fulfillment to the individual.

- Servant leaders value wholeness and growth for their followers and themselves. The power of forgiveness in Christ leads to healing and learning in their own lives, so they engage their organizations and followers in the healing quest as well.

Note that these are not a collection of random values; each strand is interwoven with the others. The value patterns result in attitudes that lead to specific actions. Robert Russell, in his work for the Regent University Center for Leadership Studies, has provided a working definition of servant leadership that illustrates the interlocking nature of these values, attitudes, and actions:

> Servant leaders *seek not to be served, but rather to serve.* They view leadership positions as opportunities to help, support, and aid other people. Servant leaders create *trusting* work environments in which *people are highly appreciated.* They *listen* to and *encourage* followers. Servant leaders *visibly model* appropriate behavior and function as effective *teachers.* They have a high degree of *credibility* because of their *honesty, integrity,* and *competence.* These persons have a clear leadership *vision* and implement *pioneering* approaches to work. Servant leaders are also conscientious *stewards* of resources. They have good *communications* with followers and exercise ethical *persuasion* as a means of *influence.* Servant leaders invite others to participate in carrying out their leadership vision. They *empower* people by enabling them to perform at their best and by *delegating* decision-making responsibilities. Overall, servant leaders provide direction and guidance by assuming the role of attendant to humanity. (Emphasis original)

Being and Doing

The influential psychologist Erik Erikson stressed identity formation. As we mature, our identity shapes our decisions and motivates our actions. The process by which human beings learn and live out an internalized identity does not lend itself to superficial description. It cannot be easily condensed into "Ten Steps Toward Becoming an Excellent Manager" or "Five Ways to Raise Great Kids." Avoid the temptation to look for a prescription. Focus instead on the attitudes and motivations behind the examples and the actions described. Think more about *becoming* than about *doing*.

We cannot transform ourselves into Christlike servant leaders any more than a mud turtle can sprout wings and teach itself to fly. Our Lord teaches that He must work the metamorphosis we need (Romans 12:1–2). In the Sacrament of Holy Baptism we have been given a new identity. The Spirit continues to work that new identity in our hearts as He integrates our thoughts and desires, shaping us daily into the image of Christ Himself. Isaiah describes Christ as the Suffering Servant (Isaiah 53). As we meditate on Jesus' great love and sacrifice for us on Calvary, we ourselves become more intent on serving others. As always, only Christ alive in us and working through the Word can do what must be done (Philippians 2:13; 2 Timothy 3:16–17).

Robert Kolb, systematic theology professor at Concordia Seminary in St. Louis, Missouri, describes this process:

Death to sin and resurrection with Christ through Baptism restores the righteousness of which Paul had been speaking in [Romans] 3–5. God freely bestows this righteousness. . . . That righteousness constitutes our fundamental identity as children of God. Sin no longer determines the identity of the baptized human creature, for it is not the constitutive or defining element of our life any longer. Christ has rendered the body of sin powerless: that is because our old selves have been crucified in our Baptisms. We no longer bear the brand of the slave-master sin, the mark of mortality. The Second Adam has triumphed over death. Because he has joined the believer to himself through Baptism, death no longer has mastery over the believer (Romans 6:6–9). (p. 36)

Christians Leaders, Servant Leaders?

As Christians, we might be tempted to claim the core values of servant leadership as "ours." After all, the command to love and serve others permeates much of the New Testament. Yet we must admit that many world religions commend the values, attitudes, and approaches prized by the proponents of servant leadership.

Can a Buddhist, for instance, become a servant leader? Yes, in one sense. Such behavior falls under the category the Reformers called "civil righteousness" or "the righteousness of reason." God has given even unbelievers the capacity to function in a moral and civil way in society. They can care for their children, support the Red Cross, and volunteer at the Humane Society. On the job, they can put in an honest day's work and even delight many with the products or services they provide.[2]

People of all faiths and of no faith have expressed interest in servant leadership as it has grown in popularity over the past decade or so. Scholars and practitioners alike have produced a small mountain of materials defining and promoting the theory. God's children find that much of this material agrees with Scripture and gives helpful insights on ways all organizations, including Christian ones, can function better. However, some theorists have generated books and articles that can potentially harm the immature or undiscerning Christian. For that reason, I do not endorse everything on the market that carries the label "servant leadership." If you decide to explore this subject outside the community of believers, stay alert.

I hope that the framework provided here will help believers—particularly those who lead Christian congregations, schools, and other organizations—build a Christ-centered understanding of servant leadership. I have attempted to integrate what the Scriptures reveal concerning Christlike leadership with the many aspects of servant leadership that are congruent with the Christian faith.

God's people can benefit from a deeper understanding of what it means to lead and follow in the church. Few Christian organizations are as healthy or well led as they might be. Many congregations chew up their pastors and lay leaders. Professional church workers sometimes abdicate their God-given leadership role or resort to overt coercion or covert manipulation. Many lay leaders have grown weary and given up on Jesus' command that His church take the Gospel into the whole world. All of us at times give in to the temptation to lead and to follow by rote, thoughtlessly unaware of the honor we have in serving the Lord Christ and His people. We also sometimes give in to an end-justifies-the-means mentality.

The values of servant leadership characterized the life and earthly ministry of our Lord Jesus. We are linked to our Lord in the bond of love He forged at the cross. We receive from Him everything we need to act out of the identity He has conferred upon us. His grace animates us. It helps us exceed the boundaries of self-discipline. It continues to work in us, even when we experience stress, fatigue, or frustration. The Holy Spirit ingrains a new identity in our hearts so that even in times of crisis we, by grace, rely on the Spirit's power and direction as we relate to those we lead—our co-workers, friends, family members, or the people in our congregation.[3]

Our Sanctifier intends to develop servant hearts in those who lead in His church and in the larger society. Why? First, so that believers can help one another grow up in Christ (Ephesians 4:11–16). Second, the Creator cares about the good of human society, and He calls Christians into leadership to advance the order, peace, and general welfare of that society (1 Timothy 2:1–3; see also *The Book of Concord*, 1959, p. 329). Finally, our Lord places some of His servants in positions of leadership in church and society so that His church can reach out in power with the saving Gospel to those who do not yet know Jesus (Matthew 28:18–20).

⫸ Where We Have Been and Where We Are Headed

We have seen that servant leadership is based in one's identity, which then shapes attitudes, values, and behaviors. While unbelievers can aspire to live out servant-leader values, Christian leaders have the supernatural comfort and strength of the Holy Spirit, transforming them day-by-day into the image of Christ. In Baptism, this indwelling Spirit has created a new identity for us. We are brothers and sisters of the risen, reigning, and serving Christ. Our Savior comforts us in our failures with His forgiveness, and He helps us in our efforts at servant leadership. To Him be all honor for what He has worked in us and through us.

The next chapter probes the first cluster of servant-leader values, attitudes, and actions—those related to service—and explains what these might look like as servant leaders, following Jesus, serve others in their organizations day-by-day.

✔ Things to Think About

Perhaps you have picked up leadership books in the past, only to find their theories hard to understand and apply. Because servant leadership is not the kind of theory that lends itself to sound-byte definitions and checklist action points, each chapter in this book will conclude with a list of questions to guide your reflection. How might the concepts presented in each chapter work out in practical terms with the members of your organization, board, or congregation? We hope the questions below will spark your imagination and perhaps provoke a discussion or two with your peers.

1. Do you see the term "servant leader" as paradoxical? Why or why not?

2. Describe a servant leader you have known personally. Why did you characterize that person as a servant leader?

3. Do you aspire to serve your organization, to lead it, or both? Listen deeply to your thoughts. What motivates your answer?

4. Skim the section headed "Being and Doing." Summarize it. How has Jesus made this real in your life?

5. Reread Russell's working definition of servant leadership. If your board, congregation, faculty, or organization had more servant leaders, what difference could it make? Why do you think so?

2

Service First!

In the early 1990s, as the Soviet empire crumbled, I traveled to Slovakia to meet with churches there as they began to set up a system of Sunday schools for their children. Under the Communist regime, the state had forbidden parents and pastors to teach the Christian faith to the young. The penalties for doing so had been severe.

Bishop Pavel Uhorskai, the leader who brought me to Slovakia, had an urgent desire to reach out with the Gospel to the young people in his nation. He had spent many years in a Soviet prison for refusing to collaborate with the Communist government. After a decade of beatings, solitary confinement, near starvation, and other brutalities, state officials "pardoned" the bishop. They advised him "in gratitude" for the pardon to move to the forests in the northern part of the country to cut timber. It was not a suggestion. Pastor Uhorskai worked for nearly 30 years felling logs for use in propping up underground coal mines.

As he told his life's story across a table laden with steaming bowls of soup, I could clearly see the deep calluses on his hands. I could also clearly see the determination in his face as his interpreter told our group that the bishop had written a fresh sermon each and every week of those four decades. Why? Bishop Uhorskai explained through his interpreter, "I never knew but what the Lord might call me to preach His Word that week." This faithful servant wanted to be ready for the Lord's call, whenever it might come.

A leader? Clearly Bishop Uhorskai was that. But in his heart of hearts, the bishop was a pastor first, a servant first—a servant of the Lord Jesus and of His people.

Service First

The more deeply one studies servant leadership, the more seeming contradictions and paradoxes one encounters. Robert Greenleaf, the practitioner who popularized servant leadership in the corporate world, once noted:

> The servant leader is servant *first*. . . . It begins with the natural feeling that one wants to serve, to serve first. Then conscious choice brings one to aspire to lead. That person is sharply different from one who is *leader* first, perhaps because of the need to assuage an unusual power drive or to acquire material possessions. . . . The leader-first and the servant-first are two extreme types. Between them there are shadings and blends that are part of the infinite variety of human nature. (*Servant Leadership: A Journey into the Nature of Legitimate Power and Greatness*, p. 13, emphasis in the original)

Greenleaf titled his first essay "The Servant as Leader." While grammar and efficiency lead us to condense the concept to "servant leadership," we do well to remember Greenleaf's original conception. Servant leaders begin by asking, "How can I help? Whom can I serve?" Then they see ways to serve by leading.

Laissez-faire Leadership?

Ken Blanchard, coauthor of the best-selling book *The One-Minute Manager*, notes that servant leadership can be misunderstood as the theory that leaders must give up leadership in favor of letting followers decide what to do and where to go. Nothing could be further from the truth. Blanchard points out that leadership involves two main functions—a visionary part and an implementation part.

All good leadership begins with a vision. Leaders set direction and inspire followers to work toward making the vision a reality. Blanchard writes:

> A river without banks is a large puddle. The banks permit the river to flow; they give direction to the river. Leadership is about going somewhere; it's not about wandering around aimlessly. . . . I want to make it clear that when we're talking about servant leadership, we're not talking about a lack of direction. Although emphasis in most servant leader discussions is on implementation, I think servant leadership involves both a visionary role and an implementation role. (pp. 22–23)

Next we consider implementation. According to Blanchard, the leader's responsibility rests on the foundation of service: "You work for your people" (p. 25). Servant leadership involves helping followers achieve their goals for their own growth and for the good of the organization. In their book *The Leadership Challenge,* James Kouzes and Barry Posner note, "Leaders don't command and control; they serve and support" (p. 16).

This kind of service orientation requires humility. It requires that the leader scrap the hierarchical paradigm that puts the leader at the top and members at the bottom. Greenleaf warns:

> The power-hungry person, who relishes competition and is good at it (meaning: usually wins), will probably judge the servant-leader, as I have described that person, to be weak or naïve or both. But let us look past the individual to the institution in which he or she serves: What (or who) makes that institution strong?

> The strongest, most productive institution over a long period of time is one in which, other things being equal, there is the largest amount of voluntary action in support of the goals of the institution. The people who staff the institution do the "right" things at the right time—things that optimize total effectiveness—because the goals are clear and comprehensive and they understand what ought to be done. They believe they are the right things to do, and they take the necessary actions without being instructed. No institution ever achieves this perfectly. But I submit that, other things being equal, the institution that achieves the most of this kind of voluntary action will be judged *strong,* stronger than comparable institutions that have fewer of these voluntary actions. ("Servant: Retrospect and Prospect," pp. 51–52, emphasis in original)

Interestingly, as Blanchard describes servant leadership, he reminds his readers of Jesus' service on behalf of His followers the night before His crucifixion. The apostle John shows Jesus kneeling to wash His disciples' dirty feet (John 13:1–17). This is not a word picture; it is not a metaphor. The water was wet and the feet were sweaty. When servant leaders see chairs to move or dishes to wash, they do not run in the other direction to search for more important, more glamorous, or more interesting tasks. Our sinful nature wants to avoid humble tasks as beneath our dignity. Scripture pictures such service as the highest honor. Jesus pronounces His benediction on our service in these words: "You know these things, blessed are you if you do them" (v. 17).

If God were to boast, of what would He boast? We would suppose the creation, the galaxies, the red giants and white dwarfs that dot His heavens. He might call attention to the miracle of life, the complexities of His one-celled creatures, the marvel of photosynthesis, the dexterity of the human hand, the delicate beauty of butterfly wings. If God were to boast, He certainly would not lack for subject matter!

We know from Scripture that He focuses on something else altogether. One of the few cases of boasting in the Bible is in Job. Here the Lord says to Satan, "Have you considered My servant Job, that there is none like him on the Earth, a blameless and upright man, one who fears God and shuns evil?" (Job 1:8).

"My servant Job." Here is God's boast to Satan! The Book of Job says much about the dark times in the lives of believers. It speaks to us about trusting our Lord even when we cannot understand Him. Yet from the beginning we catch a glimpse of the Lord's deep concern for Job, His involvement in Job's life, and the honor He has given Job—His *servant* Job. Jesus echoes this as He tells the parable of the talents (Matthew 25:14–30). Note the master's words to His two stewards, "Well done, good and faithful servant" (25:21, 23).

That title, "servant," carries a connotation of honor in both the Job and Matthew texts. We serve a great King! Even sharing a cup of cold water with a child in that King's name brings His word of commendation (Matthew 10:42). There simply are no undignified acts of service in the kingdom of our Lord.

Do your ears ache to hear your Savior say to you, "Well done, good and faithful servant"? Does your heart yearn to have your Lord boast about you as He boasted about Job? If so, you feel shame as you remember that you have not been blameless and upright. You have not always served in good and faithful ways. You have chafed under the burden of leadership, the constant demands, the thanklessness of those you lead. We are all guilty. We have not always lived up to the honor of serving others in Christ's name. But we tell our sins to God. We go to our pastor for confession and Absolution. We receive forgiveness of sins for Christ's sake. We go forth in peace and joy.

This is one of the secrets of true servant leadership in God's kingdom. As Paul says:

Not that we are sufficient of ourselves to think of anything as being from ourselves, but our sufficiency is
from God, who also made us sufficient. . . . For we do
not preach ourselves, but Christ Jesus the Lord, and *ourselves your bondservants* for Jesus' sake. For it is the God
who commanded light to shine out of darkness, who
has shone in our hearts to give the light of the knowledge of the glory of God in the face of Jesus Christ.
But we have this treasure in earthen vessels, that the
excellence of the power may be of God and not of us.
(2 Corinthians 3:4–6; 4:5–7, NKJV, emphasis added)

Only in Jesus can we claim any credentials for service, any sufficiency for leadership. Only in His forgiveness for our sins and in the righteousness He drapes
around our shoulders like a cloak can we faithfully fulfill the service of leadership. In the humility worked by
the Holy Spirit through the twin truths of our guilt and
God's grace, we receive all the other attitudes and values
servant leaders need if we want to make a lasting difference in the lives of others.

A friend of mine once taught in a Christian preschool
on the south side of Chicago. Her pastor, a brilliant
theologian with too many credentials to fit on the congregation's letterhead, spent several hours each week
in the preschool classroom. He sat on the floor to read
the children stories. He took off his jacket and finger-
painted alongside the three-year-olds. He wiped runny
noses, distributed carrot sticks at snack time, and prayed
with individual children about sick hamsters and dying
grandparents. My friend says, "He came to serve. It

seems so simple, but it made such a difference for my students and their parents."

Dietrich Bonhoeffer, a servant leader of persecuted Christians in World War II Germany, once wrote, "The renunciation of our own ability is precisely the prerequisite and the sanction for the redeeming help that only the Word of God can give to the brother" (p. 108).

Humility lies at the heart of servant leadership. True humility also lies beyond the capacity of sinful human beings. The Lord Jesus must teach our hearts the self-forgetfulness that brings us joy and the willingness to serve others (Philippians 2:13). And He does. He will work true humility in us gladly and willingly. We need only ask Him.

Vulnerability

True service means humility. It also means vulnerability. In providing leaders for His people, our Lord Jesus could have sent the angel Gabriel with a golden trumpet. He did not. He has chosen to send human leaders, sinners all, to serve in His church and in other organizations—Christian and secular alike. Leaders and followers stand together on level ground beneath the cross. When we acknowledge this, we realize that the aura of invincibility we like to wear must go.

Vulnerability includes admitting our limitations and owning our mistakes. At times we must confess indecision, confusion, and pain. James March and Herbert Simon, researchers who have explored the dilemmas of decision-making in organizations, have pointed out that no leader can know everything; we cannot control—or even predict—every result of our decisions. We serve while adrift in a sea of uncertainty. We can't do everything; there will always be more requests than resources.

Acknowledging our limitations may make us feel weak, but the truth lies in exactly the opposite direction. When we openly admit our limitations and our need for help from the Lord and other people, we allow those who follow us to use their God-given talents and gifts. Research shows that openness in this regard actually increases the level of trust in our organizations!

Some followers may find this uncomfortable. They may still insist on the leader-as-hero model. Even if we find this flattering, we need to remember that such a model easily damages both leaders and the organizations they serve. As Judith Sturnick has pointed out in her article "Healing Leadership:" "The problem with the Leader-as-Hero is that when the Hero leaves, the decapitated institution bleeds to death" (p. 192). The church, by contrast, has one head, our Lord Jesus Christ.[1] He was "a man of sorrows" (Isaiah 53:3).

Think about Jesus' vulnerability. Would you agree that He admitted the limitations of His humanity and accepted the service of others as He did His work? Jesus asked the woman at Jacob's well for a drink of water (John 4:7). He fell asleep in the back of the boat after a long day's work, leaving the disciples to navigate the Sea of Galilee (Matthew 8:24). He called the Twelve aside to rest as He grieved the death of John the Baptizer (Matthew 14:13). He accepted the financial support of many who followed Him, especially women (Luke 8:3). He wept (John 11:35). None of these actions projects a machismo image of invulnerability or a continuous grasping for control. Instead, Jesus' actions reflect the integrity of a servant leader's heart—a confident reliance on the heavenly Father and a willingness to receive the Father's help offered through the love of other people.

Often Jesus spoke with the clear authority that rightly belonged to Him. In His prophetic role, He drove the moneychangers from the temple (John 2:13–22). He rebuked the arrogant and the spiritually deaf, showing neither fear nor favor (e.g., John 10:22–39). He fully proclaimed the Word of the Lord. This illustrates the integrity of divine authority that created trust in the hearts of His followers. Yet He lived with the limitations and vulnerabilities of His true humanity. Since our Lord did this, how can we fail to admit our own human needs and limitations? How can we snap back at the admonition of others, refusing to admit our mistakes? How can we ignore our need for counsel, rest, encouragement, or accountability?

I myself live with chronic back pain, the residual effect of severe childhood scoliosis. Every so often Satan uses the pain to stir up a roiling pot of fear, anger, and discouragement in my heart. Usually in times like this I wind up in my pastor's office, looking for an ally in the battle with sin and Satan. As I pour out my frustration and rage, I have sometimes looked across the table to see tears in my pastor's eyes. That vulnerability, his willingness to feel compassion and to express it, touches me deeply. In those tears I see Jesus' tenderness and care, despite my impatience, weakness, and fury. I always find strength in the words from God that my pastor speaks, but I also find comfort in his tears.

Where We Have Been and Where We Are Headed

Servant leaders work to help others succeed. They work for their people. This kind of service requires both humility and the willingness to admit our vulnerability. Servant leaders need not fear their limitations. We have freedom in Jesus' pardon and the power to ask for forgiveness, help, and the insights of other people. Our followers do not need a superhero who stands above the fray. They don't need a paragon of virtue who always knows what to say and do. They need Christlike servants who care for them with His compassion, who serve them with His love. They need leaders whose primary identity rests in their service for Christ and His people.

As we have seen, service is a fundamental servant-leader value. In the next chapter, we will turn our attention to what Blanchard calls the "visionary role" of the servant leader. This role grows out of the value servant leaders place in helping followers find meaning and significance in their lives.

✔ Things to Think About

1. Think about a time when a deep inner sense of identity shaped your outward actions and decisions. Based on that, how would you describe the power of identity?

2. How has your new identity, given you by God as He baptized you into the death and resurrection of His Son, shaped your life? (See Romans 6:1–14.)

3. Reflect on your responses to the two questions above. Why would you advise someone who aspires to servant leadership to focus more on becoming than on doing? What does Romans 12:1–2 say regarding the power Christians need for this kind of becoming?

4. Reread Blanchard's comments in the section titled "Service." Would you describe your organization as more like a puddle or a river? Why does it matter?

5. Kouzes and Posner say, "Leaders don't command and control; they serve and support." When have you experienced command-and-control leadership? When has a leader served and supported you? Describe the results in each case. What can you conclude?

6. How can we be confident that on Judgment Day our Lord will say to us, "Well done, good and faithful servant"?

3

Servant Leaders
See Deeply

In ancient Israel, the people called the nation's prophets "seers" (1 Samuel 9:9). Those seers saw beyond outward appearances to the depths of spiritual reality. They saw beyond today into tomorrow. Because they knew the heart of God, they were also more aware of the implications of the events swirling around them in this present world.

When organizational studies today describe a leader's vision, they embrace a related concept. Today's visionary leaders can be seen as "seers" too. This is not in the scriptural sense; it means that they use natural processes to see beyond present reality to a better future. Servant leaders recognize the yearning to make a difference that lies deep within the human heart. We want our lives to count for something; we want to leave a legacy.

Remember the people of Babel after the flood (Genesis 11)? Why did they build their city and attempt to build a skyscraper that would tower into the heavens? Moses records the reason the rebels gave: to "make a name for ourselves" (v. 4).

This dishonored the Lord, as it disregarded His commands. It illustrates the lengths to which people will go to make their lives meaningful. Christian servant leaders want to harness the energy this hunger for meaning stimulates. They use their vision for the organization to provide a focus for followers' energy.

What's Your Destination?

Ships' captains want to know where they are going to go. Then they set a course that will take them there. Today's supertankers plow through the ocean with enormous power. To turn one of these monsters takes more than an hour and three or more miles of open ocean. The captain would find unnecessary course corrections less than thrilling.

Organizations are a bit like that. You don't turn them on a dime. Nor do servant leaders relish making massive, reactive course corrections with every change in tide. Instead, servant leaders set proactive goals. Leaders who do so are most likely to engage followers' commitment. As servant leaders communicate a Christlike vision in churches and in other Christian organizations, they offer followers meaning for their lives and hope for their futures. Servant leaders in the church live out of their conviction that God intended human life to have meaning and significance. Servant leaders want the people in their organizations to see the fulfillment of their dreams.

Can we square a positive, enthusiastic organizational vision with Scripture? Jesus said, "In the world you will have tribulation" (John 16:33, NKJV). He added a second promise to it, "Be of good cheer, I have overcome the world" (v. 33b, NKJV). Later on, our death-defeating Savior gave His followers a vision—evangelize the *world.* (See Mark 16:15.) Christian leaders want to avoid triumphalism—a worldview that ignores the very real power of evil and the clear teaching of Scripture that God sometimes calls His children to suffer for the sake of the Gospel. We also want to avoid a view of the normal Christian life as inevitably one of passivity, defeat, and helplessness. Both extremes distort the carefully balanced picture Scripture paints for healthy and mature believers. Hebrews 12 provides a masterful example of how leaders in Christ's church can strike this balance.

A Christlike vision offers meaning and hope. It also focuses followers' attention. Consider the apostle Paul's vision for his ministry. Jesus had healed many sick people, fed thousands on at least two occasions, cast out demons, and raised several people from the dead. After His ascension, Jesus used Paul in similar ways as His instrument of physical relief for hurting people (Acts 14:10; 16:18; 19:11–12; 28:5, 8). Even so, Paul never founded a hospital or welfare agency. He focused on the specific mission the Lord Jesus gave him—to "bear [His] name before Gentiles, kings, and the children of Israel" (Acts 9:15, NKJV).

Organizational theorist Warren Bennis uses the phrase "attention through vision" to describe the effect an engaging vision has on followers. A servant leader brings followers more than a slogan, suitable for framing in an annual report. He will use the organizational vision to focus attention and articulate goals. Servant leaders demonstrate their personal conviction that the organization's vision can become a reality. They communicate their conviction that bringing the vision into reality is exciting and worthwhile.

I recently spent a day with a group of lay people and their pastor. The meeting energized me, even though we wrestled for seven hours or so with tough questions about how to stretch resources to meet needs. Why the energy? The group never lost its focus—the Great Commission. Reaching those who don't know Jesus consumed the members' thoughts. These followers care, passionately, about the mission. Their pastor said very little for seven hours! But the discussion produced massive evidence that the Holy Spirit has used the pastor's servant leadership to burn a meaningful vision into his members' hearts—a vision for touching lives with the Gospel of Christ.

Something Old, Something New

Where do servant leaders find a vision? Do dreams, missions, callings, and purposes spring up magically overnight like mushrooms? In a sense, yes. Perhaps this explains the origin of the phrase "flash of intuition." Intuition plays an important part in developing an organization's vision. But preparation plays an essential role as well. Let's take a brief look at both.

Intuition

The role intuition plays in servant leadership can seem mysterious and unteachable. Can we cultivate or nurture intuition? Yes. Robert Greenleaf writes:

> Foresight is the "lead" that the leader has. Once leaders lose this lead and start to force their hand, they are leaders in name only. They are not leading, but are reacting to immediate events and will probably not long be leaders. . . . One is always at two levels of consciousness. One is in the real world—concerned, responsible, effective, value oriented. One is also detached, riding above it, seeing today's events, and seeing oneself in today's events, in the perspective of a long sweep of history and projected into the indefinite future. Such a split better enables one to see the unforeseeable. (*Servant Leadership*, p. 26)

Intuition in this sense grows as we listen—first to our Lord, then to our constituents, and then also to those outside our organizations. As James March and Herbert Simon have pointed out in their book *Organizations*, leaders cannot know everything. We cannot listen to everyone; we cannot pay attention to all the events unfolding around us. Studies suggest that in any given situation, human beings have the ability to take in only about 15 percent of the available data. Writing in the *Academy of Management Review*, Donald Hambrick and P. A. Mason note that leaders make decisions for their organizations based on their own highly personalized interpretations of problems, options, and outcomes. Those interpretations grow out of the 15 percent of the available data we choose—consciously or unconsciously—to consider. No wonder organizations come to reflect their leaders.

Hosea 4:9 echoes the thought that people tend to become like their leaders: "Like people, like priest." Can you see the weighty implications here for those who lead, especially in Christ's church? Can you see why leaders need to listen to the ideas and perceptions of followers, especially as leaders seek to develop insight and foresight into possible organizational futures, the organization's problems and possibilities? Can you also see how very necessary deliberate and focused attention on God's Word becomes? The Holy Spirit uses His written Word to impress upon His leaders an understanding and appreciation of the mind of Christ. This shapes and guides our subconscious interpretation of all that we encounter, both inside the church and in the world outside. King David understood the Lord in this deep way. Though David committed terrible sins, still he was "a man after [God's] own heart," one of Israel's greatest shepherd-kings (Acts 13:22).

Preparation

Visionary leaders combine their own experience with an in-depth knowledge of their organizations to derive new insights. They open windows on tomorrow for their constituents both inside and outside the organization, as they develop a vision that is rooted in the past and moving toward a better future. Such a vision has intuitive elements, but it does not spring full-grown out of nothing. A company successful at making and marketing jet skis will probably not do well if its leaders envision an organizational future building lakeside vacation homes. However, such a company might set out to build motors for racing boats or even race cars.

Servant leaders get to know their organizations and their communities thoroughly. They listen to constituents' observations, commitments, experiences, and personal goals. They ask:

- What needs do our neighbors have? How might Jesus want us to address these needs?

- What opportunities or doors has the Lord opened for us already?

- What will members or staff in this organization do even if no one pays them or notices them? What motives and dreams lie behind these voluntary commitments and actions?

- What resources could we exploit for the good of Christ's kingdom?

- How could we make a difference here as the Great Commission pulls us forward?

- What frustrates or confuses us? How could we move the roadblocks or move ourselves around them? Does Scripture have anything to say about this?

So, for instance, a congregation in the suburbs with a parish school may not be called by God to set up a soup kitchen. However, a ministry of care, teaching, and evangelism with young families may well provide a focus. And in the process of implementing it, the congregation might offer servant events such as feeding the hungry and reaching the inner city with the Gospel.

As servant leaders create and communicate an organizational vision in the church, they focus on specific and appropriate channels for fulfilling their part of the Great Commission (Matthew 28:18–20). Servant leaders tailor a vision statement for their location, given their members, expertise, and other resources. Jesus calls all congregations to carry out that commission. The Holy Spirit makes it possible for congregations to do so through a Word and Sacrament ministry.

Paul focused on the Gentiles and Peter on the Jews—both in Word and Sacrament ministries. So today congregation A may focus on ministry to students of a local university and congregation B may focus on reaching Hispanic immigrants for Christ. Will congregation B forget about its young people who go away to college? Of course not. Nor will congregation A ignore the migrant workers who move through their town twice each year. Will either congregation abandon Word and Sacrament ministry? Surely not. These means of grace are the channels by which our Lord pours His love and power into our lives. Nonetheless, since no church can do everything, servant leaders cast an intentional vision so that together, the congregation or organization can plan specific and proactive assaults on the kingdom of darkness (Matthew 16:18).

In their book *The Leadership Challenge*, James Kouzes and Barry Posner say that a vision

- presents an ideal, compelling picture of the future.

- contains no more than 25 words, preferably less, and is easily memorized.

- has enough specifics to guide an organization's decisions about which projects to take on and which to bypass.

- allows for flexibility in methods and approach as events unfold.

Venture Out!

Leaders cast a vision in preparation for action. They move their followers toward the meaningful vision they share in common. Kouzes and Posner say, "Leaders venture out." Robert Russell uses the word "pioneer" to refer to the leader's willingness to move out of the comfort zone toward a compelling vision. Greenleaf asserts:

> [A] leader needs more than inspiration. A leader ventures to say: "I will go; come with me!" A leader initiates, provides the ideas and the structure, and takes the risk of failure along with the chance of success. A leader says, "I will go; follow me!" while knowing the path is uncertain, even dangerous. (*Servant Leadership*, p. 15)

Followers derive not only a vision for a meaningful future from their leaders, but also the courage to move with their leader toward it. Servant leaders in Christ's church not only point the way toward significance in serving Christ; they dare by grace to step out front and take the lead.

⫸ Where We Have Been and Where We Are Headed

We have seen that servant leaders are servants first. They find their motivation in serving and supporting others. Nevertheless, servant leaders do not ignore their responsibility to set direction, to take risks in a pioneering spirit, and to focus the efforts of those who follow them.

An organizational focus, as we have seen, grows partly from empathetic listening to followers' hopes and hearts as servant leaders shape and communicate the organizational vision. The next chapter examines this kind of consensus through the lens of another core servant-leader value—freedom. It describes the respect leaders show for followers in building consensus and community through a Christlike use of power.

✔ Things to Think About

The questions below deal with organizational vision. If your organization has already developed a vision, concentrate your thoughts around the first set of questions. If you have not yet developed and written out a vision, concentrate on the second set. See the Appendix for sample vision statements of actual congregations. If your church does not have a vision statement, these may help you get started.

41

If you have an organizational vision:

1. In what ways did your vision arise from the hopes and dreams of your followers? How does it reflect the Great Commission? How did you listen to your Lord? How did you listen to your followers' hopes and dreams? How are you continuing to listen?

2. How thoroughly do your followers understand the organizational vision? How do you communicate your excitement and commitment? What evidence do you have that you are getting through? How often do followers hear the details of your vision? Kouzes and Posner stress the need to "keep the projector focused." Only the leader can do this for a group.

3. The apostle Paul envisioned rank upon rank of Gentile believers as redeemed and adopted children of God worshiping Jesus forever (Galatians 3:13–4:7). That vision energized his efforts and the efforts of those who traveled with him. How does your vision energize you? How do you make your vision real and concrete for your followers?

4. Cite an example of a current obstacle your organization has encountered. How might that roadblock become an opportunity? How do you help your followers identify hurdles and figure out ways to overcome them? How might your organizational vision help your followers overcome obstacles?

5. One way to call follower attention to the vision and its power is to highlight the actions of individuals who capture the vision and act on it. Sometimes

Christians have mistakenly believed that holding such people up as examples would create sinful pride in them. This may happen once in awhile. Nonetheless, the Holy Spirit inspired Paul to do it all the time. The point is, we focus on what God has done in and through people. This glorifies Him and encourages others. (See, for example, Romans 16:1–16; 2 Corinthians 8:17, 9:12; and Philippians 1:3–8.) Whom could you publicly affirm this week?

If you have not yet developed an organizational vision:

1. What value do you see in developing an organizational vision? How can you help your followers understand a vision's value?

2. In what ways will your vision arise from the hopes and dreams of your followers? How will you listen to these hopes and dreams? How will you continue to listen? Remember, followers will look to you to articulate the vision, but it cannot be yours exclusively. Nor should you listen to followers to gain approval for your preconceived notions. Listen especially to the wisdom of the mature believers in your group, and build on the insights these followers bring.

3. When will you make time to think reflectively on God's Word as you develop your vision? Why is this step crucial?

4. What part will your experiences and interests play in the vision you develop? Why is it legitimate to bring these into play?

5. How will you help your followers thoroughly understand the organizational vision? How will you communicate your excitement and commitment? What evidence will you look for as an indication you are getting through? How often will followers hear the details of your vision? Kouzes and Posner stress the need to "keep the projector focused." Only the leader can do this for a group.

4

The Power of Persuasion: Community and Consensus

Sweatshops. Child labor. The 60-hour workweek. Dirty air and foul waterways. As the Industrial Revolution developed, "progress" demanded conditions we now decry. Our forefathers endured hardship. As a result, we live more prosperous lives than any previous generation.

Until the past 20 or so years, the Industrial Revolution also dictated something else— our expectations of those who lead in organizations. As business leader Warren Bennis describes this legacy, until recently leaders were expected to COP.

Control

Order

Predict

Leaders used whatever means necessary to control the output of their factories and the productivity of their workers. Orderly little boxes, piled pyramid-like one atop the next, filled the organizational charts that graced the walls of every CEO in the western world. The captains of these bureaucracies counted on their lieutenants to keep the workers in line and fully supportive of organizational efforts. If trouble loomed anywhere on the horizon, the workers expected their leaders to fore-see it and take measures to forestall it. Control. Order. Predict. COP—Bennis chose his description with care to indicate the leader's role as one of policing, of ultimate authority, of tight supervision.

To Serve and Protect

In certain eras and organizations, the command-and-control model of leadership has worked well. Say I'm at McDonalds eating my breakfast pancakes. Customers crowd the counter. The manager barks out orders to the workers. She reassigns staff when drive-through traffic picks up. She corrects a worker who carelessly drops a basket of hash browns into a vat of boiling oil. The workers operate together like a finely tuned machine.

Still, laughter peals from the kitchen every few min-utes. The workers banter with their boss while filling orders. While the employees find themselves frustrated with the hectic pace at times and exhausted at the end of their shift, this is no sweatshop. Mechanistic orga-nizations can work with excellence and efficiency and their people can like their work.

But imagine trying to run your family like McDon-alds. The idea sounds ridiculous, because we recognize that efficiency isn't the point in families. Nobody wants a family leader who will primarily control, order, and predict. Nobody wants a "cop" in the family who will police our decisions and lay down the law, as Captain von Trapp learned from Maria in *The Sound of Music*. We want someone in leadership who will serve and protect our family, someone willing to lay down his life for the family.

The Church—Mechanistic or Organic?

If we think of fast food franchises as machines, then we might think of families as organisms. Scripture most often chooses organic metaphors to describe the church as well:

- The Bride of Christ (Ephesians 5:25–32; Revelation 21:1–19)

- The Body of Christ (1 Corinthians 12:12–30)

- The Family of God (Ephesians 3:15)

What happens when we try to import the efficiencies of machine-like organization into inherently organic groups such as families and churches? Consider Mike Michaels, chairperson of the Board of Parish Education at St. Timothy Lutheran Church. Tonight he finds himself squirming in his seat more than usual as the principal of the parish school gives his report. It's early June and three of the school's teachers have received call documents from schools in other states. None of the three has yet come to a decision about whether to stay at St. Timothy or to accept a new position in another congregation.

Mike remembers last spring and the exodus of four teachers—hard-to-replace teachers, as it turned out. Now the scenario seems to be repeating itself. Mike believes strongly in Christian education. He has worked

47

hard to communicate its benefits among parents and other members at St. Timothy. Now, he's feeling threatened.

Mike's face turns red as he slams his fist down on the table in front of him. Slowly and through clenched jaws, Mike gives the principal an ultimatum: "You tell those teachers if we don't have an answer by Monday, close of business, their silence is as good as a resignation!"

In frustration, Mike has resorted to what organizational theorists call "coercive power." Mike sees a need to predict faculty decisions for the good of the school and congregation. In order to predict, he looks for ways to control the actions of others. Mike's commitment to the shared congregational vision, while laudable, has led to a problem-solving approach he and the rest of his board will likely come to regret. The end will not justify the means. Mike has a grasp of the value of a shared vision; he does not yet understand another important servant-leader value, a value that Greenleaf calls the critical skill of servant leadership—persuasion. A friend who supervises other scientists at the Lawrence Livermore National Laboratory says, "One thing I've learned at LLNL is that if you have to invoke the authority of your position to make people do something, you effectively have no authority over them." Servant leaders realize that coercive power can damage those who exercise it, those who are manipulated by it, and the institutions that rely on it.

Power and Persuasion

Authority does have a proper place in society, as Scripture reminds us: "The authorities that exist are appointed by God" (Romans 13:1, NKJV). Without authority, society cannot function smoothly and effectively. This is also true of organizations, particularly large ones. The New Testament clearly portrays the authority Jesus Himself exercised, the authority He invested in the apostles, and the authority that God intended the pastoral office to carry:

- When Jesus had finished saying these things, the crowds were amazed at His teaching, because He taught *as one who had authority*, and not as their teachers of the law (Matthew 7:28–29).

- [Jesus said to Peter,] "I will *give you the keys* of the kingdom of heaven; whatever you bind on earth will be bound in heaven, and whatever you loose on earth will be loosed in heaven" (Matthew 16:19).

- Jesus went up on a mountainside and called to Him those He wanted, and they came to Him. He appointed twelve—designating them apostles—that they might be with Him and that He might send them out *to preach and to have authority* to drive out demons (Mark 3:13–15).

- In the presence of God and of Christ Jesus, who will judge the living and the dead, and in view of His appearing and His kingdom, I give you this charge: Preach the Word; be prepared in season and out of season; *correct, rebuke and encourage*—with great patience and careful instruction. For the time will come when men will not put up with sound doctrine. Instead, to suit their own desires, they will gather around them a great number of teachers to say what their itching ears want to hear. They will turn their ears away from the truth and turn aside to myths. But you, keep your head in all situations, endure hardship, do the work of an evangelist, discharge all the duties of your ministry (2 Timothy 4:1–5).

- The reason I left you in Crete was that you might straighten out what was left unfinished and appoint elders in every town, as I directed you. You must teach what is in accord with sound doctrine. *Encourage and rebuke with all authority.* Do not let anyone despise you (Titus 1:5; 2:1, 15; emphases added).

Those who had authority in the New Testament church seldom resorted to coercion or to attempts to control others. The model of persuasion prevailed. The apostle Paul returned Onesimus—a runaway slave—to his owner, Philemon, with these words:

- Therefore, although in Christ *I could be bold and order you* to do what you ought to do, *yet I appeal to you on the basis of love.* I then, as Paul—an old man and now also a prisoner of Christ Jesus—*I appeal to you* for my son Onesimus, who became my son while I was in chains. Formerly he was useless to you, but now he has become useful both to you and to me. I am sending him—who is my very heart—back to you. I would have liked to keep him with me so that he could take your place in helping me while I am in chains for the gospel. But I did not want to do anything without your consent, *so that any favor you do will be spontaneous and not forced* (Philemon 8–14; emphases added).

Legally, Philemon could have executed his slave, but the apostle wanted him to free Onesimus instead. Even so, Paul refrained from giving a command. He trusted the power of the Gospel at work in Philemon. Along these lines, Greenleaf suggests, "Persuasion . . . stands in sharp contrast to *coercion*—the use or threat of use, of covert or overt sanctions or penalties, the exploitation of weaknesses or sentiments, or any application of pressure. Persuasion also stands in sharp contrast to manipulation, guiding people into beliefs or actions that they do not fully understand" ("The Servant as Religious Leader," p. 159, emphasis in the original).

The desire to persuade rather than to coerce grows from the value the servant leader places on each follower's freedom, the freedom to offer meaningful service to others without compulsion. Compulsion could quickly become a side-entrance to a form of religion based on works rather than on grace. Christian leaders look to the New Testament:

• Each man should give what he has decided in his heart to give, not reluctantly or under compulsion, for God loves a cheerful giver. And God is able to make all grace abound to you, so that in all things at all times, having all that you need, you will abound in every good work (2 Corinthians 9:7–8).

- It is for freedom that Christ has set us free. Stand firm, then, and do not let yourselves be burdened again by a yoke of slavery. You, my brothers, were called to be free. But do not use your freedom to indulge the sinful nature; rather, serve one another in love (Galatians 5: 1, 13).

Referent Power

Far more than by coercive power, Jesus and His apostles led by what modern scholars have termed "referent power." This kind of power grows from the desire of others to please a person for whom they feel strong affection. Referent power usually grows slowly, over time, as followers develop friendship and loyalty toward a leader whom they admire and want to emulate. Of all the kinds of power the researchers John R. P. French and B. H. Raven identified in their groundbreaking study, referent power was shown to be the strongest. [1]

Perhaps this is so because in the case of referent power, compliance—freely given—comes from the heart. As you can see, it differs significantly from brainwashing and indoctrination. In defining leadership, Kouzes and Posner write, "Leadership is the art of mobilizing others to want to struggle for shared aspirations." Shared aspirations, as we have seen, grow from the organizational vision. Kouzes and Posner believe the words "want to" in their definition matter most. "People in positions of authority can get other people to do something because of the power they wield, but leaders mobilize others to *want to* act because of the credibility they have" (*The Leadership Challenge*, p. 31, emphasis in the original).

Followers in organizations led by Christlike servants experience a change of heart, a shift in focus from themselves to the common vision of the organic whole—the community of believers, the congregation, the family of God. No leader can coerce that kind of change. Not even Jesus Himself forced anyone to believe in Him, to follow Him, and only under very limited circumstances do Christlike servant leaders exercise coercive power.[2] Even then, control is not the goal.

Control?

I worked for much of my early business career with a servant leader who could not have cared less about controlling his subordinates. He did not insist on having his own way, though his credentials and his position in the organization gave him a great deal of authority. He never imposed his will on me and, as far as I can remember, never gave me a direct order.

He listened to me. He asked my advice again and again, when his years of experience and his education surely had given him buckets more wisdom than I could have contributed. He encouraged. And encouraged. And encouraged some more. He searched, it seemed to me, for actions or attitudes he could affirm. Whenever he saw a glimmer of such things, he wrote a note or left a voicemail message or stopped me in the hall. Because of his positional power, my mentor could have coerced.

Instead, he encouraged and affirmed. In doing so, he banked a wealth of referent power in my heart.

As a result, I paid closer and closer attention to his words. I thought about his opinions. I grew much deeper theological roots as he cultivated my understanding of God's grace toward me in Christ.

Can you see from this example the strength of referent power? Can you name anyone whose degree of control gained by means of coercion can equal the influence a mentor like this can have in someone's life?

Laying Down the Law

Let's look at this in theological terms. Coercive power relies on Law. It tells people what they should do. It incites resistance. It deflates and shames. Ultimately, the Law kills (Romans 7:9). It has no power to create vibrant, energized believers.

All of us need God's Law. Paul reminds us that the Law is "holy, and the commandment is holy, righteous and good" (Romans 7:12). Pastors who refuse to preach God's Law from the pulpit or who shy away from applying it directly to a member's selfishness or loveless actions thwart the Lord's purposes for His people. The Spirit intends that through the Law we see our need for our Savior, and we learn what pleases our Lord.

But only the Gospel message of forgiveness and peace in Jesus and His cross can motivate and animate the Christian lifestyle. Nowhere in Scripture do we see the Good Shepherd suggesting that His under-shepherds drive His people into "Christian behavior." Coerced obedience creates resentment toward God or the kind of self-righteousness Jesus condemned.

Consensus!

So what's the alternative to control by coercion? Freed from the need to control their organizations and the people in them, servant leaders can truly listen to and empathize with their constituents. They can demonstrate the patience and love of Jesus as they interact with their people and seek to lead them to consensus. Consensus flourishes in organizations when leaders show the deep empathy that listens from the heart.

Consensus means that each group member has had an opportunity to shape a group's decision and, most importantly, has committed himself or herself to making the decision work. It does not mean that all reservations or dissent has evaporated. Rather, it implies that group members have freely set aside their reservations and personal preferences in a mutual effort to implement a group decision. Individual goals have either been met or subordinated to the group's goals.

The definition of consensus given by Donald Ellis and Aubrey Fisher, respected researchers in communications theory, logically implies several things:

- Each group member has had an opportunity to share his or her thoughts and opinions.
- Others in the group, particularly those in leadership, have listened and truly heard each person's concerns.

- Each person understands and buys into the group's overarching vision and goals.

- Members have been persuaded to work together to accomplish their common goals.

Leaders forge consensus by listening to others themselves and by encouraging all group members to listen skillfully and with care to one another. To listen—really listen—is hard. Too often we

- assume we already know what the other person will say, so we tune out;

- begin planning our response instead of focusing on understanding the other person's point of view;

- fail to note the nonverbal messages connected with the words of the other person and thus miss much of the communication;

- become defensive because we feel threatened, and scramble mentally to justify ourselves;

- become impatient, because creating true consensus takes time.

These behaviors and attitudes short-circuit the kind of deep, empathetic listening that makes true consensus possible. Yet, as we overcome these destructive behaviors, our willingness to listen will benefit us and our organizations in several ways:

- Listening helps calm and comfort followers during times of change, pain, fear, and stress.

- By listening, servant leaders discover roadblocks and opportunities, needs and strengths; this knowledge makes it possible for the leader to create, communicate, and update the organization's vision and goals.

- Listening develops sensitivity to people's needs and interest, and this sensitivity builds trust in organizations.

- Those who listen to others find that others more readily listen to them.

- Listening deeply to others helps us avoid "group think," premature consensus on less-than-ideal decisions.

Empathy and Care

Do you believe that empathizing with others implies agreement with their ideas or opinions? Then empathy will come hard for you. Empathy implies not agreement, but simply understanding. Studies show that when people believe that leaders understand their points of view and concerns, they will do their best to implement decisions—even decisions with which they disagree. Grumbling and resistance tend to fade away.

Followers quickly discern a leader's motivation in listening and empathizing with their viewpoints. Do we listen in order to learn and serve? Or to control and manipulate? When we seek to serve, to serve first, followers will know it. It has been said that people don't care how much you know until they know how much you care. When we listen—deeply and with empathy— the message of care and concern comes across, whether we speak or not.

A friend of mine who has spent time in the military tells me that in the Marine Corps, the lowest- ranking personnel eat first. Those of highest rank make sure all their troops are fed before they as officers sit down to eat. This tradition underscores a critical leadership value—leaders care about their people, in deeds as well as in words.

Listening, empathy, and caring all require courage. We may learn things we don't want to know. We may uncover conflicts that make us uncomfortable. Seeing the pain and fear of others sometimes evokes pain and fear in our own hearts too.

So how can we overcome our quite natural resistance to caring and to listening too often or too deeply? We can try to drum up this courage in ourselves. We can work on becoming more self-confident. Or we can find our courage in Christ's love for us and our constituents. We can ask our Lord for a deepening confidence in His grace and power. We can meditate on our new, God-given identity as sons and daughters of the King. We can focus on what it means to know that Jesus loves His church, redeems it with His own blood, and has honored us by letting us participate in His purpose to preserve and extend His kingdom. Confident in all this, we can listen and, in doing so, "bear one another's burdens, and so fulfill the law of Christ" (Galatians 6:2, NKJV).

Where We Have Been and Where We Are Headed

In this chapter we have seen that servant leaders value followers' freedom. Consequently, servant leaders seek to serve and protect rather than command and control. They understand that organizations, particularly Christian congregations and other Christian institutions, most often thrive when leaders think of them as organic rather than mechanistic. Persuasion rather than coercion marks the servant leader's relationships with followers. Persuasion and consensus-building begin as leaders listen, deeply and with empathy, to constituents.

The next chapter introduces the idea that servant leaders steward the abilities of followers and the legacy of the organizations in which they serve.

✔ Things to Think About

1. Reflect on a time you coerced someone else into doing what you wanted. Was your approach more overt or more subtle and based on manipulation? What became of your relationship with the other person as a result? What happened to that person's ability to comply freely, from the heart? What happened in your own heart? What can you deduce from this?

2. When might coercion in a Christian organization be justified or even necessary? How can leaders protect themselves from self-deception as they use their

authority, their ability to persuade, and the coercive measures they may deem necessary?

3. Leaders cannot demand or take referent power. Followers must give it. Why is this true?

4. Think about a time someone gave you the gift of referent power. In what ways did that experience change you as a leader? What changes did you detect in the follower?

5. Create a listening action plan for yourself based on the tips listed in the section "Consensus!" Choose a specific person, a specific time and place, and a specific approach you believe will work for you. After you carry out your plan, ask yourself:

- What did I learn from the experience that will make me a better servant leader in this organization?

- What changes did I note in my relationship with the person I listened to/empathized with?

- How can I continue to derive the benefits of empathetic listening as I go about my daily leadership tasks?

5

Stewardship of God's Gifts

In the last chapter, we explored the damage a COP—Control, Order, Predict—paradigm can cause, especially in organic organizations. However, if the command and control paradigm is passe, what can take its place? Warren Bennis, who coined the COP acronym, proposes an alternative, ACE.

Acknowledge

Create

Empower

Bennis believes what many other experts in leadership have predicted—that organizations of the future will have flatter hierarchies and more cross-functional linkages. How will leaders in that kind of organization relate to others? Bennis proposes that leaders of the future will ACE as they lead.

Acknowledge

Synonyms for acknowledge might be "recognize" or "appreciate." Appreciation in turn mobilizes servant leaders to encourage and support their people. Kouzes and Posner write eloquently about "encouraging the hearts" of followers. Specifically, they advise leaders to

- build confidence in followers through high expectations. Such expectations stretch people upward to attain more than they think they can.

- show appreciation for contributions and accomplishments in ways tailored to each individual. Say thank you. Help people know that you value their dedication to the group's common goals.

- keep hope alive. By noticing and celebrating positive accomplishments and milestones along the way to those accomplishments, leaders give courage to followers. Research has shown that positive feedback increases physical stamina as well as psychological motivation!

Terry has worked with the youth at St. John for five years. When he first arrived, right out of college, only two or three high schoolers showed up for each meeting, despite the fact that more than 20 youth belonged to the congregation. Terry knew that winning these young people back would be tough. Terry's initial vision—one his pastor wholeheartedly supported—involved getting the youth back into Bible class and getting their younger brothers and sisters to participate in Bible study also, after their own confirmation. The pastor and parents alike agreed that the youth already had more than enough social activity.

Terry did many things to move toward making his vision a reality. The major strategy involved setting a three-year goal for the as-yet-nonexistent youth group: a mission trip to Mexico to build a school in a small village situated in the mountains. What a challenge! The group would need money for the trip and for building materials. They would need parental permission. They would need several adult chaperones—preferably people with carpentry skills. Most of all, they would need a thorough understanding of why they were doing such a thing and how they could share Jesus' love with the villagers while they worked.

Terry had set his expectations very high. Convincing the first three teens and their parents proved the most daunting task. That done, Terry began the uphill climb of building confidence in his plan and bringing others on board. He learned dozens of ways to express appreciation and to celebrate milestones along the way—notes of thanks, public announcements, pizza parties, articles in the congregation's monthly newsletter. It took not three years, but five—and two trips to Mexico, not just one. But after the fifth summer of Terry's ministry at St. John, the Mexican villagers had their school. Moreover, St. John had many more youth—and adults as well—participating in Bible classes and involved in several other kinds of outreach ministries.

Create

Servant leaders acknowledge and appreciate the efforts of followers. According to Bennis, leaders also create. What do servant leaders create? Communities free from fear, for one thing. Supportive environments enable followers to create workable, quality solutions to challenges and problems. Fear short-circuits follower creativity and learning.

I once belonged to a small group that got together once a week to study Scripture and pray. We also took on service projects to live out the faith we were learning. The group's leader, a pastor as well as a brilliant teacher, showed a great deal of concern and openness toward the group members. We followers responded in kind. Then the group dynamics began to change. The leader turned more and more negative. He openly ridiculed followers who misunderstood Bible texts or approached service projects in ways different from his. Soon we stopped speaking up in class for fear we would find ourselves humiliated in front of our friends. Eventually the group began to dissolve as, one by one, its members found safer ways to learn God's Word and respond to it.

Bennis writes: "Today's leaders must create a culture where ideas come through unhampered by people who are fearful" (*Managing People Is Like Herding Cats*, p. 191). Does this mean that Christian leaders never correct the half-baked notions any given follower might advance? No. But it does mean that we restore our brothers and sisters gently when that's needed (Galatians 6:1). It also means that leaders create a climate of respect for individuals and that leaders themselves model the mutual respect and love the New Testament everywhere commends.

Empower

Albert Bandura, a psychologist recognized for his development of social-learning theory, has criticized the term "empowerment" for its vagueness. Sometimes the word represents a set of action strategies, sometimes psychological states, sometimes contexts of application. Nonetheless, "It is of little value to motivate people to change if they are not provided with appropriate guides, resources, and environmental supports to realize those changes" (p. 507).

Bennis elaborates, "Today the laurel will go to the leader who encourages healthy dissent and values those followers brave enough to say no. The successful leader will have not the loudest voice, but the readiest ear. His or her real genius may well lie not in personal achievements, but in unleashing other people's talent" (*Managing People*, pp. 191–92).

Empowering others goes well beyond delegating. Both Bennis and Bandura imply that to empower others, leaders need to help followers succeed. Leaders need to equip followers with skills and knowledge, opportunities to make a difference, and individualized encouragement. They also remove obstacles to followers' success.

In the church, this equipping includes a thorough grounding in God's Word and, in particular, the fundamentals of Law and Gospel theology. It also includes elements of accountability. Servant leaders do not abandon followers simply to try to do their best. They set high standards and then make themselves available as coaches and encouragers along the way. Joe Batten, author of *Tough-minded Management* and several articles on leadership topics, says, "Servant leaders believe people are most efficient and happy when they understand clearly what results are expected of them and when they are involved in determining these results" (p. 59).

Jack Lowe, a long-time trustee of the Greenleaf Center, adds that servant leaders ask their followers the kinds of questions coaches ask:

- What am I doing that helps you succeed?

- What am I *not* doing that you need to succeed?

- Where and how am I micromanaging?

- What am I doing that you would like to do?

- When and how do I shoot the messenger?

Equipping others by sharing power with them—the power to make a difference—can achieve awesome results, especially when groups of followers are equipped in this way and then urged to tackle challenging problems.

How do we know this? Several studies have shown that the productivity of groups working on complex problems outstrips what individuals can accomplish by themselves. This finding, sometimes called "nonsumativity" or "the assembly effect," predicts that the work of a team made up of persons A, B, and C will create a better solution to a problem than they would working independently. The whole is greater than the sum of its parts. The synergy attained by combining efforts somehow enhances the final results.

Remember Terry and the youth group at St. John? Terry's group of young people, their parents, and the other interested adults in the congregation illustrate this "assembly effect." They multiplied Terry's efforts exponentially!

Terry acted as a catalyst, showing the group how—together—they could make a difference. He equipped them by providing confidence and information. Terry also gave his followers permission to act. For instance, one of his first teenage volunteers asked the shop teacher at the local high school for help. Eventually this teacher and one of his friends drew up blueprints for a simple, one-room school building and taught the youth group how to use these plans when they got to Mexico.

Terry had not known the teacher before, but instead of quashing the idea, Terry celebrated his teenaged follower's initiative. He told everyone in the congregation what the teen had done and how cooperative the teacher had been. Terry turned the teen volunteer into something of a hero. This, in turn, cemented the boy's relationship with Terry and his commitment to the mission project.

ACEs in the Church

This chapter has defined the ACE acronym in terms of practices. Remember, though, that servant leadership is values-based and is rooted in identity. Values and identity may underlie the practices of acknowledging; creating safe, stimulating communities; and empowering followers to accomplish goals. But we have not yet asked the questions: "*What* values underlie empowerment? And how do those values impact the leader's identity?" I believe the answer to these questions lies in the phrase that serves as the title for this chapter: "Stewardship of God's Gifts."

Peter Block, author of three best-selling books on leadership, has defined stewardship as "holding something in trust for another." As leaders in the corporate world interpret the value or attitude called "stewardship," they often zero in on helping their people develop their talents and abilities to the fullest potential. Maybe we should call it "optimizing God's gifts." Servant leaders in this sense do all in their power to nurture the personal and professional growth of their constituents.

Batten asserts, "Servant leaders believe and live the concept that the development of people, as a whole and in depth, pays real dividends to both the organization and the individual" (p. 48). Larry Spears, in his article "Tracing the Growing Impact of Servant Leadership," adds detail:

> Servant leaders believe that people have an intrinsic value beyond their tangible contributions as workers. As such, the servant-leader is deeply committed to the growth of each and every individual within his or her institution. The servant-leader recognizes the tremendous responsibility to do everything within his or her power to nurture the personal, professional, and spiri-

tual growth of employees. In practice, this can include (but is not limited to) concrete actions such as making available funds for personal and professional development, taking a personal interest in the ideas and suggestions from everyone, encouraging worker involvement in decision making, and actively assisting laid-off workers to find other employment. (p. 6)

How can we in the church not resonate with this and seek to excel in it? We, of all people, recognize the intimate hand of God in creating each human being with intimate care (Genesis 2; Psalm 139). In addition to these "First Article" gifts, we acknowledge that the Holy Spirit works in His church, giving gifts to each believer supernaturally, "distributing to each one individually as He wills" (1 Corinthians 12:11). Can we afford to waste any of the giftedness that God, in grace, makes available through His people? Would not doing so dishonor our Lord and blaspheme His goodness? Would it not denigrate the work of the Holy Spirit through the priesthood of all believers (1 Peter 2:9–10)?

The term "steward" originated as its users combined two old English words, "sty" and "ward." A "sty-ward" kept a pigsty. In the course of centuries the word came to describe a loftier position, that of someone who kept his lord's estate. Finally, "steward" rose to prominence as the name of a long line of English and Scottish kings. From the pigsty to the throne! Those in leadership roles who serve God's people can consider their calling to steward the giftedness of Christ's brothers and sisters a high privilege.

Risky Leadership

Empowering others to act can be risky. Consider the risks one servant leader—a perfect Servant Leader—took in an incident St. Luke records for us:

> After this the Lord appointed seventy-two others and sent them two by two ahead of Him to every town and place where He was about to go. He told them, "The harvest is plentiful, but the workers are few. Ask the Lord of the harvest, therefore, to send out workers into His harvest field. Go! I am sending you out like lambs among wolves. Do not take a purse or bag or sandals; and do not greet anyone on the road.
>
> When you enter a house, first say, "Peace to this house." If a man of peace is there, your peace will rest on him; if not, it will return to you. Stay in that house, eating and drinking whatever they give you, for the worker deserves his wages. Do not move around from house to house.
>
> When you enter a town and are welcomed, eat what is set before you. Heal the sick who are there and tell them, 'The kingdom of God is near you.' But when you enter a town and are not welcomed, go into its streets and say, 'Even the dust of your town that sticks to our feet we wipe off against you. Yet be sure of this: The kingdom of God is near.' I tell you, it will be more bearable on that day for Sodom than for that town." (Luke 10:1–12)

We need to remember that at this point in His ministry, Jesus still found it necessary to settle the squabbles that arose among the Twelve (e.g., Luke 9:46–50).

If Christ's closest followers wavered back and forth between selfishness and sanctification, can we not assume that others among His followers also suffered from sins of weakness and gaps in their understanding of the true nature of His kingdom? Still, we see our Lord commissioning workers from what we might call the "outer circle" of His followers to do real and significant work for Him.

Why take this risk? Jesus calls attention to the greatness of the harvest (Luke 10:2). He sees that the Twelve, acting alone, cannot do everything that needs to be done. The "laborers are few," He acknowledges. Based on this need, Jesus asks His followers to do two things:

- Pray for more workers (Luke 10:2).

- Go themselves as His messengers to heal the sick and announce His arrival (Luke 10:1, 9–10).

A meaningful task! A mighty trust! Think of the mistakes the 72 might have made. Think about all the many ways these messengers might have mangled the mission. And yet our Lord instructed them, commissioned them to speak and act in His name, and shoved them out of the nest. Evidently, Jesus saw learning and doing as inextricably linked. He exercised servant leadership by empowering others to pray, heal, witness, and serve. Notice the celebration when they returned:

> The seventy-two returned with joy and said, "Lord, even the demons submit to us in Your name."

He replied, "I saw Satan fall like lightning from heaven. I have given you authority to trample on snakes and scorpions and to overcome all the power of the enemy; nothing will harm you. However, do not rejoice that the spirits submit to you, but rejoice that your names are written in heaven."

At that time Jesus, full of joy through the Holy Spirit, said, "I praise You, Father, Lord of heaven and earth, because You have hidden these things from the wise and learned, and revealed them to little children. Yes, Father, for this was Your good pleasure.

"All things have been committed to Me by My Father. No one knows who the Son is except the Father, and no one knows who the Father is except the Son and those to whom the Son chooses to reveal Him." (Luke 10:17–22)

Can you see in this incident evidence that Jesus practiced the kind of appreciation and acknowledgement described earlier as characteristic of servant leaders? Jesus

- built confidence in followers through high expectations;

- stretched people to attain more than they, perhaps, thought they could;

- showed appreciation for what His followers, following His commission and filled with His Spirit, had accomplished;

- celebrated those accomplishments and stimulated hope for even greater work in the future.

An Apostolic Example

Acts 6 illustrates one instance in which the leaders of the early church empowered followers to help them carry out the Great Commission.[1] The harvest of souls continued to ripen after Pentecost. Too few workers had entered the fields. The apostles took the initiative in asking the church to appoint seven deacons to begin a ministry of care for the poor so that the apostles themselves could continue in prayer and in the Word and Sacrament ministry Christ had entrusted to them.

It would be wrong to think of servant leadership as a way to use people in a manipulative way to achieve one's own self-interested purposes. Yet it would likewise be wrong to let the gifts and abilities of God's people waste away, underdeveloped and underappreciated.

Following our Lord who sent the 72, and imitating leaders in the early church who appointed the deacons, servant leaders in Christ's church today consider themselves stewards, caretakers, of the gifts God gave to their constituents. They help those around them acknowledge, develop, and use their unique gifts. This will advance the kingdom of Christ. Our Lord wants His people to use their gifts and abilities because doing so enriches our lives:

> One of life's greatest and most meaningful laws is the paradox that we cannot find ourselves until we have first of all lost our lives in some service or wholehearted endeavor. This is actually true of the Christian life. Jesus says, "Whosoever would save his life shall lose it; and whosoever shall lose his life for My sake shall find it."

. . . And what a life it is! It is the abundant life. (John Herrmann, *The Chief Steward: A Manual on Pastoral Leadership*, p. 14)

Stewardship of Organizational Legacies

Servant leaders see themselves as stewards or caretakers of their followers' gifts. However, servant leadership operates at the institutional as well as the personal level. Servant leaders exercise stewardship over the institutions they serve. Servant leaders in the church recognize the value of the organizational legacy inherited by God's servants in the present from God's servants in the past.

Robert Greenleaf describes two alternatives, both ultimately destructive. First, one can consider the flaws and imperfections in existing institutions and simply retreat. Such a person withdraws meaningful support and chooses to act, if at all, outside "the system." Or one can attempt to reform an existing institution. Noticing that those initial efforts have failed to result in instant perfection, a leader may decide to destroy the institution completely so that a new and perfect institution can grow up in its place. Greenleaf wryly comments, "Not much thought seems to be given to the problem of where the new seed will come from or who the gardener to tend [it] will be" (*Servant Leadership*, pp. 10–11).

Neither the perfect congregation nor the perfect denomination nor the perfect Christian organization exists—at least not here on earth. Eugene Peterson, in his book *Working the Angles: The Shape of Pastoral Integrity*, writes:

> The biblical fact is that there are no successful churches. There are, instead, communities of sinners, gathered before God week after week in towns and villages all over the world. . . . In these communities of sinners, one of the chief sinners is called pastor and given a designated responsibility in the community. The pastor's responsibility is to keep the community attentive to God. (p. 2)

A particular Christian organization may need to change. A given congregation may need reform. The needed change may be drastic. But servant leaders recognize the wisdom of first discerning where the weight-bearing walls stand, lest they find themselves alone in a pile of rubble their carelessness has created. Greenleaf notes, "The servant, in my view, is generally a gradualist" ("Servant: Retrospect and Prospect," p. 44).

Servant leaders consider the past as they plan for the future. Buoyed up by the heritage of their institutions and riding on the shoulders of those leaders who have served before them, today's servant leaders innovate to meet the challenges of the future.

Where We Have Been and Where We Are Headed

In this chapter we have considered an alternative to the Control, Order, and Predict paradigm—Acknowledge, Create, and Empower others. The ACE approach grows out of a recognition that servant leaders are stewards of the gifts our Lord has placed in His people. Empowering others has its risks—risks that Jesus Himself took as He sent the 72 to work in His name. But our Lord took those risks so that His followers could have the joy of a fulfilled, abundant life. Servant leaders today seek that same fulfillment for their followers. Servant leaders also have stewardship of the institutions they serve; they value the legacies they have inherited.

In this book's final chapter, we will consider the ongoing need for growth and healing that leaders, followers, and organizations alike share. We will look for ways to create "safe places" in organizations so that all organizational members can risk, learn, and encourage one another in the forgiveness and acceptance Jesus has made possible.

✔ Things to Think About

1. What challenges do you personally find in the ACE approach to leadership?

2. Does receiving appreciation from others enhance your ability to serve? Why might some leaders hesitate to acknowledge others or to express appreciation? How would you counter these reasons?

3. Think about a supportive community in which you have participated. What did the leader do to create or sustain the sense of support you experienced? How did that support help you and others contribute

creatively to the group's goals? What clues does this give you as you think about your own leadership?

4. Despite all the evidence that empowering people produces positive results, leaders sometimes hesitate to do it. What have you observed in this regard in others? In yourself? Do any of the arguments in this chapter nudge you forward toward empowerment? Explain.

5. What new insights did you gain as you read about Jesus sending the 72 from Luke 10? What attitudes and core beliefs impelled Him to do what He did in this instance? Which of these values do you share? In what specific ways might your organization or congregation change if you practiced these values even more intentionally than you do now?

6. What legacy have you inherited in the institution you now serve? For what parts of that heritage are you most thankful? How can you as a servant leader honor and steward the heritage you have received while not letting it paralyze you as you challenge your people to face today's concerns?

6

Growing and Healing

A fire station in my community displays a sign near the front door. It depicts two large hands that surround the figure of a small child, as if protecting her. The sign has two words: "Safe Place." Anyone—particularly any child—who gets lost, hurt, or fearful can come to the fire station to find help and safety.

Think for a moment. Could you hang that sign on the front door of your church building? Or near the entrance of your organization's meeting rooms? Or next to your own office? How would others in your congregation answer those questions? How do you know?

Organizational Nervous Breakdowns

Peter Senge, noted expert in organizational learning, writes about today's "massive institutional breakdowns on an unprecedented scale." He comments:

> It is hard to find any institution in modern society—business, government, public education, the family—that is not suffering breakdown. . . . Many people seem to believe that technology is the major driver of change. . . . Personally, I think that *only the most superficial changes are being brought about by technology.* . . . The really big issues facing mankind concern our inability to understand and manage our complex human systems.

. . . We are out of control, driving down a dark road with little or no light, and most technological progress amounts to speeding up. (pp. 123–25; emphasis in the original)

After Senge describes the problems of the present and the future in this kind of graphic detail, he goes on to prescribe an antidote. He does not ask us to pop two aspirin and call his consulting firm in the morning. Like Robert Greenleaf, Senge refuses to point leaders to a new gimmick or this week's quick fix. The problem, as he sees it, is profound, and the remedy must be too. Senge calls for

- more reflective thought on the part of leaders;

- more "systems thinking" by organizations (i.e., more awareness that our environment—in both its physical and social aspects—is interconnected; every action in one part of the system affects every other part);

- more attention to the quality of our interpersonal relationships;

- more intentionality in developing places of safety in our organizations so that people can feel free to grow, to experiment, to make mistakes, and to learn.

This chapter will refer to each of these four points several times as it explores the fifth and last servant-leader value given in chapter 1:

Servant leaders consider the processes of forgiveness, healing, and learning as necessary in their own lives and in the lives of those they serve. In light of this, servant leaders work toward personal balance and wholeness for themselves, and they find ways to engage their organizations and followers in the healing quest as well.

Our Shadow Selves

Senge urges, "Don't leave learning to chance" (p. 133). Still, as he later notes, leaders often do just that. Why? For one thing, much of the time, learning means change. Machiavelli first observed, "Change has no constituency." Many times, even leaders who understand the need for change have trouble embracing it with zest. Senge also calls for more reflective thought on the part of leaders. Yet many of us resist reflective thought. Why do many human beings often find both reflective thought and change so difficult?

My local public library has hundreds of audionovels, along with dozens of nonfiction titles. I check out a stack of these whenever I plan to drive long distances. I like to listen to old-time radio programs most. The characters take on a life of their own in my mind. Someday I'd like to meet The Shadow. Few of us, though, relish a real-life encounter with our own "shadow side," as researchers Lawrence Lad and David Luechauer call it:

> [As] you journey toward becoming a servant-leader you will likely uncover some things about yourself that you may not like, might not want to encounter, and would rather not know. For example, are you really ready to share control, can you be humble, are you capable of uplifting others . . . ? [The] process . . . may likely force you to question some of your most cherished assump-

tions about yourself, others, and the nature of organizations. You might not like the answers you find. (p. 65)

No wonder few leaders think. No wonder we don't examine the quality of our interpersonal relationships. The shadow self deep within us knows what we suspect when we're fully awake—our lives and our relationships are not altogether moonlight and roses.

Warren Bennis describes this shadow side as the gap between who we are and who we should be. He urges leaders to blame no one, but instead own up to the gaps and accept responsibility for them. He further recommends that we keep alert to our own defensiveness, analyzing what may lie buried beneath it.

Confess and Be Healed

Christian leaders won't argue with any of this. We recognize in the words of these secular writers faint echoes of Christian truth. Keep in mind the incongruities you've already noticed as you think about the words of 1 John 1:8–9, "If we claim to be without sin, we deceive ourselves and the truth is not in us. If we confess our sins, He is faithful and just and will forgive us our sins and purify us from all unrighteousness."

The original Greek word for "confess" is *homologeo* (*homo*—"same"; *logos*—"word"). It means "to speak together" or "to say the same thing." When we confess our sins to God, we face our shadow self head-on. We set aside our defensiveness and our tendency to deny our faults. When done on a regular basis, reflective thought, led and empowered by the Holy Spirit, brings believers to the point of contrition—a recognition of sin and sorrow for it. We agree with God that

- our attitudes, words, actions—or all three—have been wrong;

- our behavior has hurt us and those around us—family, church, and community. We have brought more pain into the world of hurt in which we live;

- we have, by our sin, damaged the quality of our relationships;

- we have, by our sin, snapped off the safety that makes growth, learning, and peace possible for ourselves and others.

Denial minimizes sin. Denial says, "It can't be that bad." Denial blames others. Denial says, "He did it too" or "She did it first." Denial avoids taking responsibility. Denial claims, "I can't help it; I got irritated." Denial pops another pill, pours another drink. Denial bursts out at others in fits of rage. In contrast, God's Spirit says, "Come. Confess. My presence is a safe place for you to pour out your guilt, your shame, your pain, your failure. Here is healing. Here is pardon. Here is strength. Here is the cross of Christ, raised on Calvary's hill for you."

Cycles of Renewal

Judith Sturnick works with servant leaders in the process of healing and notes that they often need help moving beyond what she calls "seductive cycles of grief" and into "constructive patterns of renewal" (p. 189). Servant leaders can get stuck in their guilt or in feelings of failure and find it hard to move back into the mainstream of a productive, other-focused life. Many of Sturnick's clients don't make it.

Maybe you've known Christian leaders who struggled in "seductive cycles of grief." Maybe you have found yourself trapped in such a vortex. I once worked with a teacher who wrestled with what she called her "ghosts"—memories from a painful past that kept her from enjoying her work in the present. She agonized over project after project never feeling anything she did was good enough. She habitually missed important meetings. She pulled all-nighters for a week or so before each quarter's grade cards came out, trying to write the perfect set of anecdotal comments for each student. Her Christian service was painful to watch.

Our Lord has not left us without recourse. He holds out to us His help for breaking through the cycles of grief Sturnick describes. For example:

- The familiar practices of the liturgy—Scripture lessons, words of confession and Absolution, songs of praise to the Savior, the real presence of Christ in the Holy Supper—become for us conduits of grace stretching from heaven to earth. Here is help. Here is healing from heaven.

- The regular practice of private confession and Absolution can calm the vortex of feelings often associated with guilt—shame, grief, anger, depression, hopelessness. Ask your pastor about this comforting rite.

- God has also given us gifts through what we might call "First Article channels"—the work of medicine and psychology. Since Adam and Eve sinned, human faculties have all been less than fully functional. Low levels of neurotransmitter chemicals in the brain can lead to biologically based depression that prayer alone may not alleviate. My faculty friend, caught up in the spiral of self-deprecation, found help and healing for herself and her family through a Christian counselor and antidepressant medication.

In all these ways our Lord comes into our lives to heal and help. His presence is the "safe place" to which servant leaders can find rest, encouragement, and strength for further service. While healing is seldom easy from a human standpoint, the safety and acceptance Christ offers His believers does make continual renewal possible. James writes, "Confess your sins to each other and pray for each other so that you may be healed. The prayer of a righteous man is powerful and effective" (5:16). Here our Lord promises to pour out into our lives the fresh streams of healing that flow from the fountain of forgiveness that He opened for us in His death and resurrection. He invites us to pray for one another, promising that our words will ascend to heaven with power and great effect. Where else can servant leaders find such a power source for the renewal we need as we continue to serve our Lord and His people?

Organizations and Denial

Organizations or, more precisely, the followers in them also need to engage one another in the "constructive patterns of renewal," as Sturnick recommends.[2] How can servant leaders help generate this process of organizational healing? How can we help our institutions face up to their own "shadow side"? How can we lead members to acknowledge the spiritual dangers of perfectionism . . . the illusion of organizational infallibility . . . the lie that it's okay to expect flawless performance from their leaders and fellow members? How can we help our followers come to grips with ambiguity?

I sat one evening with a congregational task force, gathered to evaluate an ongoing midweek Bible study program for adults. The group as a whole and the individual leaders in it had put a lot of time and energy into developing the program, finding guest instructors, publicizing throughout the community the courses being offered, planning a wide-ranging curriculum, and so on. During the first semester more than 70 learners participated. Now, two years and six terms later, only about 25 people were enrolled.

As our discussion began, group members rehearsed the vision we had shared in our initial planning stages. We mulled over details and raised questions.

- What if we offered a light supper before class? Or maybe just bagels?

- Have we fallen down in our publicity efforts?

- What if the classes ran a few weeks longer? Or shorter?

The conversation took a darker turn as it progressed. At this point, group members seemed to look around for someone to blame for the enrollment decline. Comments like these arose.

- People let themselves get too busy with things that aren't important.

- No one will sacrifice anymore.

- We don't have a "Bible study culture" here.

- Having one of the worship services at the same time that Sunday school meets has taught people to ignore Bible class options.

After about 20 minutes or so of this venting, the tone switched again. In a more subdued mood, participants voiced more questions.

- Have we prayed consistently against Satan's schemes to keep people away from hearing God's Word?

- Have we relied too much on sociological approaches or "marketing methods"?

- Have we maintained a Gospel motivation rather than a Law-centered motivation as we invited participation?

After a while this soul-searching brought the group back to a more hopeful stance again as the focus shifted away from ourselves to the promises of the Lord Christ. One group member, a kindergarten Sunday school teacher, mentioned a parable Jesus once told. It began to disperse the discouragement as we shared its promise with one another:

> This is what the kingdom of God is like. A man scatters seed on the ground. Night and day, whether he sleeps or gets up, the seed sprouts and grows, though he does not know how. All by itself the soil produces grain— first the stalk, then the head, then the full kernel in the head. As soon as the grain is ripe, he puts the sickle to it, because the harvest has come. (Mark 4:26–29)

The group prayed and left shortly thereafter. As I drove home, I reflected on the skill the leader used as he gently guided the meeting.

- At first, he allowed people to tiptoe around the issues, to warm to one another, and to test the water to see if this was, indeed, a "safe place" to air genuine thoughts, questions, and feelings.

- Then, as frustration, anger, and disappointment began to surface, the leader let members share those feelings. He did not leap in with instant admonitions or "spiritual" quick-fixes. He let the poison drain away before he brought out the salve and bandages.

- As the self-examination then began anew—on a spiritual level this time—nods of recognition passed from person to person as we informally confessed to one another the sins of self-reliance and the neglect of prayer we each saw in our own lives. The leader let this happen. He did very little prompting, but he did use listening skills to draw everyone out.

- Finally, nudged by the promise of the parable, the group began to hope again. The leader pointed out this change, this hopefulness produced by the Gospel. He reminded us we could return to use the spiritual weapons of warfare God has given us through Christ (Ephesians 6:10–18). At this point, we also began to plan fresh ways to publicize and to adjust program mechanics to make the classes more accessible to more members.

The term "healing process" can sound complex, scary, or beyond the capacity of most leaders in the church until you consider that healing often happens as simply and as naturally as it did for this task force. Confident in the power of the Gospel, the leader listened and helped us face our failures and the ambiguities of the task we had set for ourselves. Then he led us back to the hope that is ours in Christ's cross. As I have watched, reflected, and learned over the years, I have come to believe that this is the essence of the healing process in the church. Greenleaf notes:

> The best prescription, it seems to me, is to *listen intently*, with the genuine wish to learn without judging every motive, every attitude, every reason. And one must regard what one hears—which may not be pretty in some cases—as manifestations of illness to be healed rather than error to be corrected. It is amazing what problems will melt away when all one does is listen intently, with the attitude of healer. It is possible for a parent to take the heat out of a child's temper tantrum in a matter of seconds by listening. . . .

If you see the impediment to group effectiveness as *illness,* you have a chance to enter the relationship as *healer,* as one who seeks to make whole—to make everybody whole, including yourself, the healer—so that *all* may see more clearly where they should go and how to get there. I am not arguing the general proposition that there is no error that needs to be changed or corrected. My only point is that it is a sounder attitude to enter the person/team relationship as a healer rather than a change agent. Not only is it a more effective approach, but one is less likely to fall into the trap of playing God. ("Types of Leaders," pp. 92–93, emphasis in the original)

This kind of listening and gentle leading captures the essence of the "healing presence" that Christlike leaders who are servant leaders bring to their organizations. Leaders care and listen—deeply. But only Jesus can heal!

Learning for Leading

The process of spiritual healing takes place whenever the Gospel of grace, the Good News of God's forgiveness in Christ, is proclaimed—whether formally in the liturgy or informally as I have described it above. This process carries great power and promise for servant leaders and their organizations. We need to recognize the need for other kinds of growth. Some of the "gaps" Bennis notes are not sin at all, but instead gaps in knowledge or insight. Perhaps we find our communication style failing again and again. Perhaps our attempts at expressing appreciation for what others do seem to fall flat. Perhaps our people don't exactly want to be empowered. What can a servant leader do then?

Organizations share these kinds of knowledge gaps with their leaders. That means everyone—the leader and the led—must be fully engaged in the process Senge calls "organizational learning." David Garven, in his writings for the Harvard University Business School, has identified three steps to the organizational learning process:

- *Acquiring needed information.* This includes separating relevant from irrelevant data—knowing what to listen to.

- *Interpreting information.* This involves avoiding distortions brought about by our own biases or preconceived notions.

- *Applying what we know.* If organizations don't act on what they have learned, they have wasted the time and effort it took to gather and interpret the information in the first place.

Many books, audiodiscs, articles, and other resources available today—such as those cited in these pages—deal with organizational learning. No matter how you and your organization choose to address your need to learn, you will find that you need freedom to experiment with new ideas, approaches, challenges, and options. When safe places for learning exist, leader and followers together grow more relaxed in the face of ambiguity. They accept the limitations and potential for failure that often mark life in this world. This, in turn, tends to foster a healthy balance in the lives of leaders and followers.

Walking the Balance Beam

Picture a funeral pyre blazing against the night sky. Watch the flames leap and dance into the darkness. Now imagine yourself flinging your friendships, your health, your family, and your capacity for joy and fulfillment into the flames. Servant leaders everywhere at some time or other will find themselves facing the temptation to stack everything on the altar of "dedication" or "commitment." Organizations too often encourage this kind of behavior in leaders and followers alike. Sometimes the organization will even light the match!

A supervisor living out this warped view of commitment once told me, "All your time is this congregation's time." Guilt-evoking beliefs like this, combined with the concern all servant leaders carry in their hearts for those they serve, can easily lead to the kind of "compulsive activity" that Fassel calls workaholism. The servant leaders she counsels believe, deep down, that "if I weren't active, I would have no right to exist" (p. 219). Diane Fassel, author of *Working Ourselves to Death*, cites three myths that feed the flames of this dysfunctional approach to life:

- Myth 1—Workaholics are more productive. Activity equates with productivity.

- Myth 2—No one ever died of hard work. My body has no limits.

91

- Myth 3—The stress-reduction techniques I've learned will erase any ill effects of over-working.

Fassel counters each of these myths with facts drawn from research and her own clinical experience. Studies have shown that activity does not necessarily correlate with productivity. Medical research likewise tells us that our bodies do indeed have limits. They will succumb to any of several stress-related illnesses if we do not properly care for them. Stress-reduction techniques will work—but only to a point. After we reach that point, we're only kidding ourselves. Besides, no stress-reduction technique in the world will patch together a broken relationship with a spouse or child who has suffered neglect for months or years.

Here we come back to Senge's concern for systems thinking and for attention to the quality of our interpersonal relationships. Leaders in the church may find themselves tempted to overwork, overeat, skip exercise, burn the candle at both ends, and ignore the very human need for love and friendship. They should consider St. Paul's words of concern and counsel, "Do you not know that your body is a temple of the Holy Spirit, who is in you, whom you have received from God? You are not your own; you were bought at a price. Therefore honor God with your body" (1 Corinthians 6:19–20).

All of our time is God's time. But our bodies are God's bodies as well. We do not honor God by sacrificing one for the other. Both must be kept in balance by the wise steward. How will this recognition and a Christ-honoring attitude work itself out in the day-by-day life of a servant leader? How can we help our organizations to see their responsibilities in this regard? Sturnick urges servant leaders to

- work toward understanding and honoring boundaries. Help your followers do the same.

- let go of perfectionism in your own life. Show your followers perfectionism's pitfalls as well.

- look for creative ways to deal with uncertainty and ambiguity in both your own work and in the organization's mission.

- foster an attitude of experimentation in your own life and in your organization. Help followers understand the old adage that the only people who don't make mistakes are those who never do anything.

- maximize the benefits of unexpected discoveries and surprises.

In *The Power of Servant Leadership*, Larry Spears writes, "One of the greatest strengths of servant leadership is the potential for healing one's self and others. Many people have broken spirits and have suffered from a variety of emotional hurts. Although this is a part of being human, servant-leaders recognize that they have an opportunity to 'help make whole' those with whom they come in contact" (p. 4).

As our Savior lived here on earth, much of His ministry was a ministry of healing. He healed broken bodies, to be sure. But He also healed broken hearts. As those who follow us see our own growing willingness to admit our ongoing struggle with our sins, our failures, our vulnerability, our need to grow in knowledge, our commitment to balance in our lives and to reasonable self-expectations, they may find the courage in Christ to do the same.

The concept of healing as a process should not sound foreign to those who lead in Christian settings. It describes the essence of the process theologians call "sanctification." Martin Luther addressed this need for continued healing, even among those who lead Christ's people: "This life, therefore, is not righteousness, but growth in righteousness; not health but healing; not being but becoming; not rest but exercise. We are not yet what we shall be, but we are growing toward it. The process is not yet finished, but it is going on. This is not the end, but it is the road. All does not yet gleam in glory, but all is being purified" (p. 31).

God bless you, my brother, my sister, as you heal and as you lead!

✔ Things to Think About

1. For whom is your church a "safe place"? For whom might it not be? How do you know? How could you find out?

2. What gets in your way as you attempt to incorporate more of each of these in your life?
   - Reflective thought
   - Systems thinking

- More attention to the quality of your personal relationships
- Freedom to make mistakes and learn from them

3. In what sense is the Christian life an ongoing process of healing and growth? In what sense is our relationship with Christ a finished, settled reality? How do each of these answers lead us as believers to hope and peace?

4. Think about a specific time when you found yourself stuck in what Sturnick calls a "seductive cycle of grief." How can this prevent further growth? What processes does the Lord most often use to break these cycles in your life? What can you learn from this that might be helpful as you lead in your organization?

5. Have you or your organization bought into any of the three myths Fassel identifies as contributing to workaholism? Cite the evidence on which you base your answer. How might an individual or an organization begin the process of recovery in this aspect of our service for Jesus?

6. What specific plans do you have to facilitate your personal growth as a servant leader in each of these facets of your life? How will you build accountability into your plan?
   - Spiritually
   - Emotionally
   - Relationally
   - Intellectually

Appendix

This section contains several sample mission/vision statements taken from the Web sites of congregations affiliated with The Lutheran Church—Missouri Synod. Different congregations use different terms to refer to their vision statements, but all intend that the statement they develop will guide their ministries into the future. I have chosen representative statements; you, of course, will want to craft your own based on your specific circumstances. See chapter 3 for further help.

As you examine these mission statements, you may want to keep Kouzes and Posner's criteria in mind. (See pages 40 – 41.) Not all of the mission statements below fulfill these criteria exactly. Even so, you may find the samples helpful as you think and pray about your own congregation's vision for mission.

Statements

We have been called to faith and life in Jesus Christ, the son of God . . .

- To minister in Christian love to one another.
- To grow through Christian discipleship.
- To follow the Savior's command to make disciples of all nations through the faithful proclamation of God's Word.

St. Paul Lutheran Church, Chicago Heights, IL

Our Mission as God's people at Trinity is to grow in our commitment to Jesus Christ and to one another so that we can be used by him to bring the saving Gospel to everyone!

Trinity Lutheran Church, Kalispell, MT

— We exist to grow in our relationship
  with Jesus and with one another.
— We accomplish this by learning, worshiping, sharing, and praying.
— We strive to bring others into a relationship with Jesus and with us.

King of Glory Lutheran Church, South Elgin, IL

In accordance with God's Plan, and inspired by the love of Christ, we at Our Savior Lutheran Church are compelled to share the message of God's salvation with all people through a Spirit-led and caring worship, education, fellowship and service so all may grow in a personal relationship with Christ.

Our Savior Lutheran Church, Livermore, CA

Loving, serving and sharing Jesus with *you*!

Immanuel Lutheran Church, Michigan City, IN

In the name of the Lord we worship and serve in this community and, by sending others, throughout the world. Depending on God to enable us, our purpose is . . .

To bring people to Christ.
To strengthen people in Christ.
To maintain people with Christ.

Village Lutheran Church, Ladue, MO

Our mission is to reflect the compassionate heart of Jesus, by ministering to the needs of individuals and families. We want to spread the Good News of Salvation, making disciples of Jesus Christ, in the power of the Holy Spirit, through Word and Sacrament.

Messiah Lutheran Church, Missoula, MT

The explicit mission of Immanuel Lutheran Church and Immanuel Christian School is *to share the hope of Jesus Christ* in and through the corporate celebration of Word and Sacrament, the faithful preaching of God's Word, confessional religious instruction, genuine caring, fellowship, and diligent evangelical outreach, that all people, within the sphere of our influence, may come to the knowledge of Salvation as it is revealed to us in the Holy Scripture.

Immanuel Lutheran Church, Manchester, NH

The people of Holy Cross see as their purpose serving our Lord Jesus Christ, caring for the spiritual and physical needs of the community, and sharing God's Love and Grace by providing worship, education and fellowship opportunities for all.

Holy Cross Lutheran Church, Mahwah, NJ

To Connect People to Christ
and Together Grow in His Word

Christ Lutheran Church, Lincoln, NE

To comfort those in need, reach the lost, and build the body of Christ by proclaiming the truthfulness of God's Word in love.

Redeemer Lutheran Church, Newton, NJ

The mission of Our Savior Lutheran Church is to live in response to God's love for us in Christ through spiritual growth in worship, fellowship, witness, education, spiritual care, and loving service to God's people and all our neighbors.

Our Savior Lutheran Church, Sedalia, MO

Share God's Word, Share His Love, and Do It Now!

Christ Lutheran Church, Norfolk, NE

To reach the lost people in the city of Milwaukee with the power of the Gospel of Jesus Christ:
- To bring salvation to everyone.
- To transform the believer by beginning to heal their hurts.
- To build a loving, caring community where faith, hope and love are lived and demonstrated.

Gospel Lutheran Church, Milwaukee, WI

Yesterday, today, and until Jesus comes again—preaching and teaching the Word of God for the salvation of all believers.

Hanover Lutheran Church, Cape Girardeau, MO

Notes

Chapter 1

1 Milton Rokeach, in *Beliefs, Attitudes, and Values: A Theory of Organization and Change*, first distinguished between "instrumental values" and "terminal values." Instrumental values deal with preferable conduct; terminal values focus on desired end states of existence. I have chosen to state the servant-leader values listed here as terminal values, because I believe the many lists of instrumental values associated with servant leadership can be subsumed under them.

2 Of course, civil righteousness earns no one right standing before God—only through faith in Christ Jesus does God impute to us the righteousness Jesus earned for all people through His cross and resurrection. Even unbelievers can understand and champion the values of servant leadership. Rodney Stark, in *The Rise of Christianity*, admits that the spread of the Christian faith brought with it a concern for individuals unlike anything seen before. Greenleaf and others want to broaden the theory so that leaders and organizations worldwide can benefit from its tenets. Even so, one can argue that apart from the Judeo-Christian ethic, the values of servant leadership might not have developed.

3 This underlying theological foundation also lifts the ideal of servant leadership above New Age techniques and human-potential doctrines promoted by the popular-press business literature. Human potential practitioners espouse many of the values and have used some of the language of servant leadership. Even so, Christians who carefully discriminate between truth and error based on God's revelation in the Holy Scriptures can find much of value in the servant leadership literature. A full discussion of the

human potential movement and its influence in our society lies outside the scope of this booklet. For further information, consult Eldon Winker's book *The New Age Is Lying to You*.

Chapter 2

1 Likewise, our Lord heads the Christian organizations that support the work of the church.

Chapter 4

1 Several researchers have defined "taxonomies of power." French and Raven identified coercive power (the ability to punish), reward power (the ability to reward), legitimate power (authority bestowed by one's position or office), expert power (expertise, unique knowledge or experience), and referent power (defined above).

2 Lord Acton wrote, "Power corrupts and absolute power corrupts absolutely." Greenleaf comments: "It is interesting to note that Lord Acton, a Catholic layman, made this statement in heated opposition to the assumption of papal infallibility in 1870. And what is the corruption that . . . Acton might have had in mind? I believe it is arrogance, and all of the disabilities that follow in the wake of arrogance" ("Servant: Retrospect and Prospect, p. 47).

Chapter 5

1 A thorough exegesis of the Acts 6 text lies beyond the scope of this booklet. I have discussed the office of the Holy Ministry and related offices in the church at some length in *Go and Make Disciples: The Goal of the Christian Teacher*. See also "The Ministry: Offices, Procedures, and Nomenclature" (1981), a report of the Commission on Theology and Church Relations of The Lutheran Church—Missouri Synod, also available from Concordia Publishing House.

Chapter 6

1 Sturnick warns readers that toxic organizations can dishearten and even destroy servant leaders. She urges leaders not to protect or rationalize destructive—we might say sin-

ful—organizational behavior. Not all organizations want to heal! Furthermore, Sturnick insists that leaders caught up in toxic organizations explore their reasons for remaining there. She warns that healthy people in sick organizations begin to act in unhealthy ways just to survive. This can seriously compromise the leader's ability truly to serve and to foster healing. Even in the church, leaders sometimes must, in grief, shake the dust from our feet, as Jesus said (Matthew 10:14). Our departure in such cases serves as our final word of Law to those who rebel against His grace.

2 Several good books can help you or your followers understand the importance of establishing and maintaining healthy boundaries. See, for instance, Henry Cloud and John Townsend, *Boundaries: When to Say Yes, When to Say No, To Take Control of Your Life* (Grand Rapids, Mich.: Zondervan, 1992).

References

Bandura, Albert. *Self-efficacy: The Exercise of Control.* New York: W. H. Freeman and Company, 1997.

Batten, Joe. "Servant-leadership: A Passion to Serve." In *Insights on Leadership: Service, Stewardship, Spirit, and Servant-Leadership*, edited by Larry Spears, 38–53. New York: John Wiley and Sons, 1998.

Bennis, Warren. *On Becoming a Leader.* Reading, Mass.: Addison-Wesley, 1989.

_____. *Managing People Is Like Herding Cats.* Provo, Utah: Executive Excellence Publishing, 1997.

Blanchard, Ken. "Servant-Leadership Revisited." In *Insights on Leadership: Service, Stewardship, Spirit, and Servant-Leadership*, edited by Larry Spears, 21–28. New York: John Wiley and Sons, 1998.

Block, Peter. *Stewardship: Choosing Service over Self-Interest.* San Francisco: Berrett-Koehler, 1993.

Bonhoeffer, Dietrich. *Life Together.* San Francisco: Harper, 1954.

Burns, James McGregor *Leadership.* New York: Harper and Row, 1978.

Cline, Roberta J. "Detecting Groupthink: Methods for Observing the Illusion of Unanimity." *Communication Quarterly* 38 (1990): 112–26.

Ellis, Donald, and Aubrey Fisher. *Small-group Decision-making: Communication and the Group Process.* 4th ed. New York: McGraw Hill, 1994.

Erikson, Erik. *Dimensions of a New Identity.* New York: W. W. Norton, 1974.

Fassel, Diane. "Lives in the Balance: The Challenge of Servant Leaders in a Workaholic Society." In *Insights on Leadership: Service, Stewardship, Spirit, and Servant-Leadership*, edited by Larry Spears, 216–28. New York: John Wiley and Sons, 1998.

French, John R. P., and B. H. Raven. "The Bases of Social Power." In *Group Dynamics: Research and Theory*, 2d ed., edited by Dorwin Cartwright and Alvin Zander, 607–23. New York: Row, Peterson, 1960.

Frick, Don. "Understanding Robert K. Greenleaf and Servant Leadership." In *Insights on Leadership: Service, Stewardship, Spirit, and Servant-Leadership*, edited by Larry Spears, 353–60. New York: John Wiley and Sons, 1998.

Fryar, Jane. *Go and Make Disciples: The Goal of the Christian Teacher.* St. Louis: Concordia Publishing House, 1992.

Garven, David. *Learning in Action: A Guide to Putting the Learning Organization to Work.* Boston: Harvard Business School Press, 2000.

Goldhaber, Gerald M. *Organizational Communication.* 6th ed. Boston: McGraw-Hill, 1993.

Greenleaf, Robert. "Types of Leaders." In *Seeker and Servant*, edited by Anne Fraker and Larry Spears, 89–100. San Francisco: Jossey-Bass, 1996.

_____. *Servant Leadership: A Journey into the Nature of Legitimate Power and Greatness.* New York: Paulist Press, 1977.

_____. "Servant: Retrospect and Prospect." In *The Power of Servant Leadership*, edited by Larry Spears, 77–92. San Francisco: Berrett-Koehler, 1998.

_____. "The Servant as Religious Leader." In *The Power of Servant Leadership*, edited by Larry Spears, 111–67. San Francisco: Berrett-Koehler, 1998.

_____. "Religious Leaders as Seekers and Servants." In *Seeker and Servant*, edited by Anne Fraker and Larry Spears, 9–48. San Francisco: Jossey-Bass, 1996.

Hambrick, Donald, and P. A. Mason. "Upper Echelons: The Organization as a Reflection of Its Top Managers." *Academy of Management Review* 9, no. 2: 193–206.

Herrmann, John. *The Chief Steward: A Manual on Pastoral Leadership*. St. Louis: The Lutheran Church—Missouri Synod Department of Stewardship, Missionary Education and Promotion, 1951.

Kolb, Robert. *Making Disciples, Baptizing: God's Gift of New Life and Christian Witness*. St. Louis: Concordia Seminary Press, 1997.

Kouzes, James, and Barry Posner. *Credibility: How Leaders Gain and Lose It, Why People Demand It*. San Francisco: Jossey-Bass, 1993.

_____. *The Leadership Challenge*. San Francisco: Jossey-Bass, 1995.

_____. *Encouraging the Heart*. San Francisco: Jossey-Bass, 1999.

Lad, Lawrence, and David Luechauer. "On the Path to Servant Leadership." In *Insights on Leadership: Service, Stewardship, Spirit, and Servant-Leadership*, edited by Larry Spears, 54–67. New York: John Wiley and Sons, 1998.

Lowe, Jack. "Trust: The Invaluable Asset." In *Insights on Leadership: Service, Stewardship, Spirit, and Servant-Leadership*, edited by Larry Spears, 68–76. New York: John Wiley and Sons, 1998.

Luther, Martin. *The Works of Martin Luther*. Vol. 3. Edited by Theodore G. Tappert. Philadelphia: A. J. Holman, 1930.

March, James, and Herbert Simon. *Organizations*. New York: John Wiley and Sons, 1958.

McCollum, Jeffrey N. "The Inside-out Proposition: Finding (and Keeping) Our Balance in Contemporary Organizations." In *Insights on Leadership: Service, Stewardship, Spirit, and Servant-Leadership*, edited by Larry Spears, 326–39. New York: John Wiley and Sons, 1998.

Melrose, Ken. "Putting Servant Leadership into Practice." In *Insights on Leadership: Service, Stewardship, Spirit, and Servant-Leadership*, edited by Larry Spears, 279–96. New York: John Wiley and Sons, 1998.

Morgan, Gareth. *Images of Organizations*. Thousand Oaks, Calif.: Sage Publications, 1998.

Peterson, Eugene. *Working the Angles: The Shape of Pastoral Integrity*. Grand Rapids: William B. Eerdmans, 1987.

Pugh, Derek, and David Hickson. *Great Writers on Organizations*. Omnibus ed. Dartmouth: Dartmouth Publishing, 1993.

Rokeach, Milton. *Beliefs, Attitudes, and Values: A Theory of Organization and Change*. San Francisco: Jossey-Bass, 1969.

Russell, Robert. "Exploring the Values and Attributes of Servant Leaders." Unpublished manuscript, Regent University—Center for Leadership Studies, 1999.

Schein, Edgar H. *Organizational Culture and Leadership*. 2d ed. San Francisco: Jossey-Bass, 1992.

Senge, Peter. "Through the Eye of the Needle." In *Rethinking the Future*, edited by Rowan Gibson, 122–46. London: Nicholas Brealey, 1998.

Sheehy, Gail. *New Passages: Mapping Your Life across Time*. New York: Ballantine Books, 1995.

Spears, Larry. "Tracing the Growing Impact of Servant Leadership." In *The Power of Servant Leadership*, edited by Larry Spears, 1–12. San Francisco: Berrett-Koehler, 1998.

Stark, Rodney. *The Rise of Christianity*. San Francisco: Harper, 1997.

Stone, Gregory, and Bruce Winston. "Theory S: A Values-based Theory of Management and Leadership Focusing on People and Results." Unpublished manuscript, Regent University—Center for Leadership Studies, 1998.

Stubbs, Irving. "A Leverage Force: Reflections on the Impact of Servant Leadership." In *Insights on Leadership: Service, Stewardship, Spirit, and Servant-Leadership*, edited by Larry Spears, 314–21. New York: John Wiley and Sons, 1998.

Stueber, Ross. "The Characteristics of an Effective Lutheran High School Administrator." Ph.D. diss., St. Louis University, 2000.

Sturnick, Judith. "Healing Leadership." In *Insights on Leadership: Service, Stewardship, Spirit, and Servant-Leadership*, edited by Larry Spears, 185–93. New York: John Wiley and Sons, 1998.

Winker, Eldon. *The New Age Is Lying to You*. St. Louis: Concordia Publishing House, 1994.

Yukl, Garry. *Leadership in Organizations*. 4th ed. Upper Saddle River, N.J.: Prentice-Hall, 1998.